Coaching Business Builder

Workbook and Planner

Putting the Pieces Together

Potentials Realized Media
Newmarket | Toronto | Muskoka
Ontario, Canada

Jennifer J. Britton

Coaching Business Builder Workbook and Planner
Putting the Pieces Together

Jennifer J. Britton

Published by
Potentials Realized Media
Newmarket | Toronto | Muskoka
Ontario, Canada

Copyeditor: Clarisa Marcee, www.AvenueCMedia.com
Cover and Interior Design: Davis Creative, www.DavisCreative.com

ISBN: 978-0-9937915-3-6

Quantity discounts are available on bulk purchases of this book for educational, gift purposes, or as premiums for increasing magazine subscriptions or renewals. Special books or book excerpts can also be created to fit specific needs. For information, please contact Potentials Realized, PO Box 93305 Newmarket, Ontario, Canada L3X 1A3.

Dedicated to all those who dream about "What's Possible?" and take the leap to create what they want through their business. A big thank you too, to those "who have our backs" and are there to support us through the ebbs and flows.

Contents

Acknowledgments vii

Introduction 1

Section 1 | Business Fundamentals—The Foundations Overview 3

    The Current State of the Profession 6

    Different Coaching Models—What Are You Offering? 6

    Different Coaching Business models 7

    Business Mix 7

    Developing Your Skill and Craft as a Coach 10

    Our Clients 13

    Your Ideal Client 13

    Knowing Your Client Profile 15

    One of Our Most Important Resources—Ourselves 15

    Not Reinventing the Wheel 19

    To-Do and Not-To-Do Lists 20

    The Iceberg—Our Mindsets, Behaviors, and Results 23

    Business Fundamentals 28

    Core Business Fundamentals Metaview 30

Section 2 | Solopreneur Primer 31

    Vision 35

    Be True to Who You Are 36

    Strengths and Flow 39

    Reflection Questions: 43

    Don't Just Do It Once (Mastery, Repurpose, and Republish) 43

    Collaboration 47

    Ingredients for Collaboration: 49

    Get Out There 51

    Lead and Serve 55

    Client Preferences 56

    Have Fun and Do What You Like 58

    Creating Undeniable Value 59

    What Do Your Client's Value? 60

    Continuous Learning—Keep Fresh 62

    It's All Yours! 64

    End-of-Section Checkpoint 65

Section 3 | Marketing Essentials 67

Developing a Business Plan 69

Five Essential Coaching Business Systems 70

Promotional Vehicles—Beyond Social Media...76

Building Visibility—Web and Online Presence 87

Finding an Accountability Partner..88

Phases of the Co-Facilitation Journey: 89

Social Proof and Other Testimonials...90

End-of-Section Checkpoint 92

Section 4 | The Ecosystem.. 93

Business Vision..95

Vision Timeline...97

Strengths 98

THE SWOT—Looking at Your Inner and Outer Context......................................101

Bringing It All Together—The Ecosystem 103

Keys for Business Success..110

Time Management and Personal Productivity for the Business Owner....................114

End-of-Section Checkpoint 122

Putting It Into Action...122

Section 5 | The Planner 125

Annual Planning Tools..129

Quarterly Planning Tools...135

Monthly Planning Tools 145

Content Planner...243

The "Back Pages"—Creative Tools 273

Acknowledgments

As a solopreneur for more than 14 years now, I have valued the varying partnerships which have allowed me to scale the impact and results of my work. This book is no different. *The Coaching Business Builder* has been forged by thousands of hours of business coaching and conversations with coaches at all stages of their development. Whether you are in day 1 or day 1,000 of your business, I trust that there will be several questions for you to take forward.

I want to thank a number of colleagues who took the time to review the initial version of this workbook, and who provided encouragement to get this out in the world today.

As always a big thanks goes to my family. They are the primary driver for WHY and HOW I run my business, and the mark I want to make in the world. At the same time, they are a tremendous support for me in enabling me to do the work that I love.

A thank to you for the leadership of Janica Smith on this second publication under the Potentials Realized Media banner. She and her team of Clarissa Marcee, and Jack Davis have moved this project quickly forward. A big thank you!

A thank you as well to these initial reviewers: Michelle Mullins, Janice Cummings, Molly Rose Teuke, Melissa Burns, and Latifu Munirah. Your comments and insights helped catalyse this creative project.

Thank you to Lindsay Dunphy who spent many hours helping to piece together many of the earlier materials I had created.

The roots of the Coaching Business Builder started back in 2004, when I was engaged as a part time business faculty member at a local post-secondary institution to teach Human Resources, then Preparing a Business Plan, Marketing and other foundational business topics. For the next five years I found myself working and speaking significantly on small business and entrepreneurial issues, just as I was building my own thought leadership in group and team coaching.

In fact, some of my earliest group coaching groups were with small business. The 90 Day Biz Success™ program ran quarterly for many years, and in 2010 I started offering it as a program license to coaches. In the last eight years many coaches have taken this forward with their own clients, and I continue to hear the value they have received. In 2007, I started running my first business planning virtual retreats, which really lay the foundation for the planner and Section 4—The Ecosystem of the book.

Today in 2018 it's exciting to see how my work has come full circle. The seeds of this workbook and planner come from the dozens, if not hundreds of hours I have spent leading Virtual Business Planning Retreats since 2007, and the many, many group and individual coaching conversations I have had with coaches.

I trust that you will find this journey useful, regardless of where you are in your own business development it's designed to get you to pause and take stock of where you are at. Whether we are in month one, or year 15, or thinking about stating a coaching business, the CBB will get you to consider a variety of coaching questions.

Today's VUCA context is Volatile, Uncertain, Complex and Ambiguous. It's a context where things are changing radically and rapidly, and "good enough" has become the mantra.

While the workbook and planner could touch on a wide variety of additional topics, I trust that this WILL BE ENOUGH to get you going.

Enjoy and I hope that our virtual paths will cross soon! Please let me know how I can support you in your coaching journey.

Best

Jennifer

Jennifer Britton – Potentials Realized

May 2018: Toronto, East Gwillimbury and Muskoka, CANADA

Introduction

Welcome to the Coaching Business Builder! Over the past fifteen years I have had the opportunity to work with hundreds of coaches at all stages of their business development. From pre-start up when people were contemplating the shift out of a full-time job, to start up, to experienced coaches.

This book is part workbook, part planner. It's meant to cover many of the foundations you will want to explore as you put your business together, or, take it to the next level.

This book is divided into five sections:

Section 1—The Foundations of Building a Coaching Business

Section 2—The Solopreneur Primer

Section 3—Marketing and Promotional Essentials

Section 4—The Ecosystem—Exploring your own internal, and external, terrain

Section 5—The Coaching Business Builder Planner—An undated series of planner pages to support you for the next 12 months

The sections can be tackled one at a time, or you may find yourself pulled to certain sections at the different development stages of your business.

You are encouraged to grab a pen and write as you go through the book, as it is designed as a workbook, and prompt to get you thinking.

When I launched my own business in 2004, I was hungry for practical tips and ideas to help me envision and create my business. I devoured books, engaged in coaching for my business, and immersed myself in sharpening my coaching skills. I also quickly got things into action, launched, tracked, experimented, tracked, and acted again. I had to. My bank account was dwindling.

I think that one of the most important things I've done over my career as a leader and entrepreneur has been to take consistent action. Throughout the book, I'll be sharing some of my own stories so you can learn from the experimentation I've undertaken, where things have worked, and where some haven't.

In addition to being a workbook designed to support you in reflective pause, and planning, this book is part annual planner. Monthly, quarterly, and annual planning tools are geared to support you in thinking about what you want to do, scheduling it, and getting it done! Like most things, cultivating a business requires consistent effort and focus, and my hope is that this becomes a go-to resource and tool for you.

Let's get started!

Section 1

Business Fundamentals— The Foundations Overview

This section explores the foundations of running a coaching business. In this section we are going to explore several aspects of launching and growing a coaching business:

The Context of Coaching Today
- Current State of the Profession
- Different Coaching Models

Business Mix
- What Are You Offering?
- The Funnel

Skills and Strengths for Coaches
- Wheel of Small Business Mastery
- Developing Your Skill and Craft as a Coach
- ICF Core Coaching Competencies

Your Clients
- To Niche or Not to Niche?
- Client Profile

Our Most Important Resource—Ourselves
- Being Selective
- Understanding our key business drivers and motivators
- To-Do and Not-To-Do Lists
- Experimentation
- Change and Ongoing Development
- The Iceberg of Mindset
- Your Vision

Business Fundamentals
- Cash Flow is King
- The One-Percent Rule to Business Development

In tandem with this, some of you might find yourselves pulled to Section 4 on Ecosystem. Do take a look!

The Context of Coaching Today

The Current State of the Profession

According to the 2016 ICF Global Coaching Survey, there are 53, 300 professional coaches working globally who generate $2.356 billion US in revenue each year[1].

As a profession, coaching can be traced back to the early 1990s. There are many types of coaches—executive coaches, parent coaches, life coaches, divorce coaches, business coaches. There are one-on-one coaches, team coaches, group coaches. The nuances between the different types of coaches is beyond the scope of this book; however, all coaching branches share common methodology and philosophies, namely:

- The client (the person(s) being coached) sets the agenda
- Clients are naturally creative, resourceful, and whole
- Coaching is a future-focused conversation
- Coaches work in partnership with the client
- Goals, action, awareness, and accountability are key parts of any coaching conversation

In his report, *Executive Coaching 2022*[2], Brian Underhill, founder of Coach Source and specialist in the design and management of enterprise-wide executive coaching services, highlights several trends we are likely to see as the profession grows more sophisticated: 1) Leadership development programming being supported by coaching, 2) *Leader-as-coach training* (training leaders in organizations on coaching skills), and 3) *Team coaching*—coaching individual members of the team and/or developing that team *as a team*.

Different Coaching Models—What Are You Offering?

Given the diversity of what coaching can look like, you will want to start by looking at what you are offering. Are you creating a coaching practice that focuses on one-on-one coaching? Or are you building a company that offers coaching along with other services? Is this a side gig or a full-time business?

Coaching is part of the service-based industry, and many coaches offer products, books, e-books, and online courses, in addition to coaching and other services (training, facilitation, consulting).

Recent research from the ICF has found that coaching professionals span the coaching continuum[3]:

Coach practitioners including:

- External coach practitioners
- Internal coach practitioners
- Both internal and external coach practitioners

Coaching skills have also taken root among non-coaching management professionals, including:

a. Human resources/talent development managers and directors who use coaching skills

b. Managers and leaders who use coaching skills

---

1 https://coachfederation.org/app/uploads/2017/12/2016ICFGlobalCoachingStudy_ExecutiveSummary-2.pdf (downloaded 5.15.18)
2 https://coachfederation.org/blog/21025-2
3 ICF Coaching Survey 2017

You will want to check out the *2017 Global Coaching Consumer Awareness Study* from the ICF, which explores questions such as:

- How do different generations access coaching?
- How do views on coaching vary?
- What is the value of coaching?

Different Coaching Business models

There is a wide range of different coaching business models. From the traditional one-on-one coaching delivery business model to a model that incorporates individual, team, and group-coaching support, there are also business models grounded in passive revenue.

Unlike trading dollars for hours, passive revenue in a coaching business can create an ongoing revenue source to even out the peaks and valleys of cash flow. Passive revenue usually includes books, digital products, on-demand programs, or program licensing—things that "sell while you sleep."

Your business is yours! It can be as complicated, diverse, or as straightforward and streamlined as you would like.

Each coach is likely to have their own business model and as you move through this workbook, you are going to get a sense of what some of the possibilities are. Your business model will be different from mine, and possibly different from others you trained with. Regardless, I'd like to explore some basic foundations common to most business models.

Business Mix

What's Your Business Mix?

The term "business mix" refers to those items you have included as part of your revenue streams. For coaches this could include:

- Individual coaching services
- Group coaching
- Team coaching
- On-demand programming—video-based courses, e-courses
- Other passive revenue products—cards, workbooks, books
- Virtual programs

The Funnel

In building a coaching business we may have different services and offerings at different levels—from free to high-end services. Consider what you are offering at the different levels and note them on the following page. When you are ready, note the price range of each product or service.

As you complete this exercise, what do you notice? What services currently exist? What do you want to create?

_____

_____

Skills and Strengths for Coaches

As service-based business owners, we want to **leverage what we're great at**. We also want to build on our strengths. As coaches, many of us are solopreneurs, so we are a "one-person show." Or we may have a very small team, often a virtual team, behind us. We explore strengths further in Section 2.

Given this scale, we may be required to develop a lot of skills in running our business. From **administration** skills, to **marketing** skills, **program or product development**, to **people management**, *along with* coaching.

Coaching skills are just one of the skill sets, which will help a business flourish. If we don't bring these additional skills, we will also need to make sure that someone on our team brings them. If we don't have a team, hopefully, we can grow these skills or leverage the strengths of others.

Wheel of Small Business Mastery

The Wheel of Life is a popular coaching tool. It has been adapted here to form the Wheel of Small Business Mastery to get you thinking about the holistic context of business development. Consider where you are on a range of 1-10 (with 1 being low and 10 being high) in each of the following small-business elements:

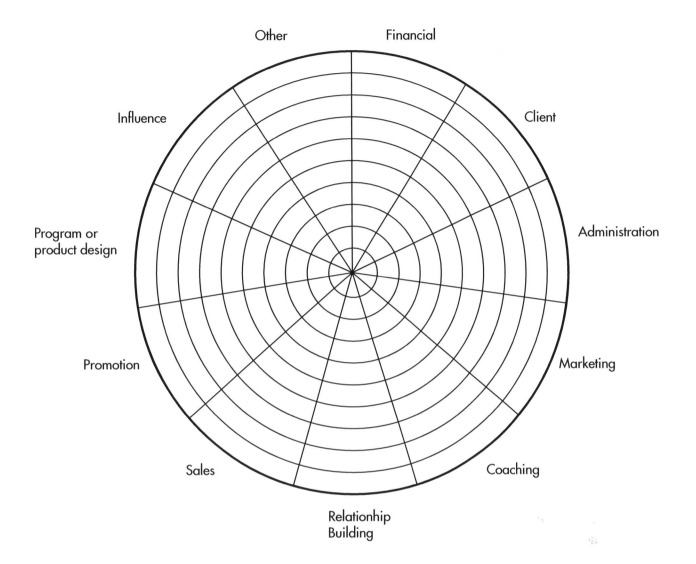

Area	My Score (1-10)	Notes
Financial		
Client		
Administration		
Marketing		
Coaching		
Relationship Building		
Sales		
Promotion		
Program or product design		
Influence		
Other		

We will be exploring many of these different areas in the coming sections.

Activity: As you reflect on your Wheel:

Make a list of the different areas you want to put attention around.

_____

_____

What areas do you think you will need support in?

_____

_____

What possible source will provide the needed support?

_____

_____

Developing Your Skill and Craft as a Coach

As a practitioner coach myself, I hold the bias that coaching skills are refined through the art of conversation. If we are not in conversation, our skills and presence as a coach, can atrophy and wither.

The development as a coach is an ongoing one. It's as important to continue developing our skills in year twelve as it is in year two. The context of our clients is ever-evolving, calling us as coaches to do things differently and learn things ourselves. We coach our clients, not in a vacuum, but in an ever-evolving context. Knowledge of this context is not essential to be a great coach, but it is important in understanding the reality in which they operate.

In developing our skills as a coach, we want to make sure we are continually evolving as a coach. Despite the myriad coaching models and methodologies springing up year after year, grounding all of them are the ICF Competencies. As a mentor coach myself, I appreciate the layers of interconnection across the competency base.

Whether we are coaching individuals, groups, or teams, the competencies remain the same, even though they may look and sound different. Some coaches—team and group coaches, for example—may find that they require additional skills, for example, knowledge of group and team process, to be masterful in their work.

The ICF Competencies

Using the ICF Competencies as a guide, you'll notice that in coaching—whether you are coaching an individual, group, or team—we are leading from 11 core skills, encapsulated into four main areas. Take a look at the following chart to note what skills you are good in and what areas you might want to further refine.

A. Setting The Foundation

3. Meeting Ethical Guidelines and Professional Standards

4. Establishing the Coaching Agreement

B. Co-Creating the Relationship

5. Establishing Trust and Intimacy with the Client

6. Coaching Presence

C. Communicating Effectively

7. Active Listening

8. Powerful Questioning

9. Direct Communication

D. Facilitating Learning and Results

10. Creating Awareness

11. Designing Actions

12. Planning and Goal Setting

13. Managing Progress and Accountability

(From the International Coach Federation: www.coachfederation.org)

Using the Coaching Business Builder, you have an opportunity to take stock of your skill set as a coach.

In recent years the notion of supervision has emerged as an important part of our profession. Both junior and seasoned coaches can benefit from stepping back, pausing, and reflecting on what they are doing as a coach.

Take a few minutes to read through the 11 core coaching competencies of the International Coach Federation, their definition, noting the different approaches and techniques you use as a coach. Also, give yourself a rating on the different skill areas. What do you notice?

Competency	Definition-ICF	Core Approaches/ Techniques	Rating on a Scale of 1-10 (1=low, 10=high)
A. Setting the Foundation			
Meeting Ethical Guidelines and Professional Standards	Understanding of coaching ethics and standards and ability to apply them appropriately in all coaching situations		
Establishing the Coaching Agreement	Ability to understand what is required in the specific coaching interaction and to come to agreement with the prospective and new client about the coaching process and relationship		

Competency	Definition-ICF	Core Approaches/ Techniques	Rating on a Scale of 1-10 (1=low, 10=high)
B. Co-creating the Relationship			
Establishing Trust and Intimacy with the Client	Ability to create a safe, supportive environment that produces ongoing mutual respect and trust		
Coaching Presence	Ability to be fully conscious and create spontaneous relationship with the client, employing a style that is open, flexible, and confident		
C. Communicating Effectively			
Active Listening	Ability to focus completely on what the client is saying and is not saying, to understand the meaning of what is said in the context of the client's desires, and to support client self-expression		
Powerful Questioning	Ability to ask questions that reveal the information needed for maximum benefit to the coaching relationship and the client		
Direct Communication	Ability to communicate effectively during coaching sessions, and to use language that has the greatest positive impact on the client		
D. Facilitating Learning and Results			
Creating Awareness	Ability to integrate and accurately evaluate multiple sources of information, and to make interpretations that help the client to gain awareness and thereby achieve agreed-upon results		
Designing Actions	Ability to create with the client opportunities for ongoing learning, during coaching and in work/life situations, and for taking new actions that will most effectively lead to agreed-upon coaching results		
Planning and Goal Setting	Ability to develop and maintain an effective coaching plan with the client		
Managing Progress and Accountability	Ability to hold attention on what is important for the client, and to leave responsibility with the client to take action		

Overall, what do you notice? What are the 2-3 areas you want to put attention around?

_____

_____

_____

Our Clients

We exist in a business to serve others. Our clients will shape how, and when, we work and what we offer. This section explores—To Niche or Not to Niche as well as the Client Profile.

To Niche or Not to Niche?

As a junior coach and new business owner, I constantly heard how important it was to niche…AND I knew that my former world of work had been one as a cross-disciplinarian where I was a "Jill of All Trades." A typical week in my former career found me working across healthcare, education, disaster management, micro-enterprise, and team development. For me, the idea of niching and focusing only on one client group seemed restrictive.

A niche is defined in the Oxford Dictionary as: "denoting or relating to products, services, or interests that appeal to a small, specialized section of the population."[4]

Niches are beneficial because:

- They provide a focus on one type of client
- They allow us to develop a range of products or services in that area to meet the needs of that group
- They enable us to specialize and go deep into one area
- Coaches can develop a reputation in that area

The downside of niches is:

- Coaches may become disconnected with other influences and trends occurring
- Coaches may feel constrained that this is their only area of focus
- Over time, there may be fatigue or burnout from working with one type of client

There is a multitude of research from organizations such as Gallup, pointing to the importance of individuals and other professionals being able to bring their strengths to work every day. As a solopreneur, a challenge is about being or becoming well rounded. So, if we find that we are struggling in certain areas of our business—like accounting—maybe it's a flag to explore what it would take to bring someone on board. Perhaps a virtual assistant or an accountant, could help you run and manage your business finances.

Your Ideal Client

Figuring Out Who Your Client Is—The Client Profile

Our clients will shape everything from what we offer, to when we offer it, to *how* we offer it. Whether we have a wide span or "neighbourhood," or the smaller span of one niche, getting to know your client pays off.

---

4 https://en.oxforddictionaries.com/definition/niche. Accessed 5.22.18

One of the most popular questions I get asked is, "How do I learn more about my prospective client?" There are many ways. You might do this by asking questions to current clients, pulling together a focus group of prospective clients, hosting a table at a trade show or speaking at an industry conference. These are all marketing and relationship-building strategies to get to know your clients.

One tool available to you here is the **Knowing Your Client Profile.** For more than a decade now I've been asking coaches who are planning group coaching to consider these questions as they go to design programming for their own clients. These are also the questions that I have been asking myself as I've gotten to know different clientele over the years.

Always start off with a **broad description of who is the client.** Is it a stay-at-home mom? Is she a millennial entrepreneur who wants to get things going, who is ramping up her startup, and wants to sell it at a million dollars plus?

What **are the client's needs?** What are some of their main goals? Use the worksheet to write down the top three goals you see for this type of client.

What's keeping them up at night? In some sales processes this is known as the "pain point." What has gotten to the point at which they are ready and willing to do something about it, by investing money and time?

What are the things you can help with as a coach? We're not there to solve the issue, we're there to partner and support clients to solve their own issues. What are the top 2-3 issues you can support them on?

What is the age range you want to work with? Are they a Gen Z or millennial? Are they a Gen Xer or are they a Boomer? What about their gender and their socio-economic status? Geographically, where are they based? What is their professional status? Are they a business owner so they have free reign in spending, so they don't have to go through a budget approval process? In contrast, do they have once a year to make a pitch for services for support?

What are their spending patterns? When is money available? Business owners may not have money available at tax time, and leaders may not have money available in the new year unless they have budgeted it.

What's the lead time to that business decision? Are they likely to see something today and sign up right away, or do they need to go to someone to get approval?

What is their availability? When do you think they will want to access services? Is it morning? After work? Weekends? I know that on Mondays it's a great time to catch business owners who want to engage in masterminds, but it's not a great time to engage with professionals in other areas, especially team leaders.

Learning and interaction today can take many forms. A provocative question to always be exploring is, "Is coaching what's really needed?" How often do you explore this with clients and organizations you work with? What other supports would be of benefit to your clients? You might consider training, mentoring, or other supports.

What associations and organizations do they belong to? Marketing and building relationships with the organizations your clients are part of is another marketing strategy. I'll be getting into this a little bit later. It can be useful to look to associations to help you connect with their members, understand the issues that are important to them, and also become a trusted partner or service provider.

What are **people's preferences**? If this client were to come together, where would they like to congregate, where would they like to meet with you? Face to face? Virtual? Would they prefer the intimacy of a sit down, face-to-face coaching session or are they located halfway around the world and want to meet you via skype while they're going to bed and you're waking up? This is what's wonderful about our business and work as coaches. We can coach from almost anywhere.

Finally, what's been your own personal experience with the group? What else do you know about them?

Before moving on, I'd like you to take some time to think about your clients: *who are they, what do they need, and what's important for them.*

Take a few minutes to complete the Knowing Your Client Profile. After you look at that, note the gaps between what you know and what you don't. Note any research you want to undertake.

Knowing Your Client Profile

Broad description	
What are their needs?	
What are their goals?	
What keeps them up at night?	
What are the issues they are looking for support around?	
Age range	
Preferences	
Spending patterns	
Lead time to decisions	
Availability	
What other supports might they want? (Is coaching what's needed?)	
Associations and organizations they belong to	
Preferences for meeting or accessing products and services	
Personal experience with the client group	
Other	

Research I want to do:

One of Our Most Important Resources—Ourselves

As a business owner, there's a lot of work we may do around ourselves. In this section, we are going to look at:

Being selective

Understanding our business motivations or drivers

Cash flow is king

Being consistent

Not reinventing the wheel

To-Dos and Not-To-Dos Lists

Experimentation

The iceberg

Identifying key business values and behaviors

Being Selective in Doing the Work We Want

Another business fundamental is about being **selective**. Many coaches are surprised once their business is established that they hit their ceiling and fill their capacity pretty quickly. At this point, you may need to turn work away—even work you'd love to do. What is the work *you REALLY want to be doing*?

Depending on your business model, whether you are coaching one-on-one, whether you're doing groups, there is an upper threshold of how many people we can serve, based on our time and our outreach models.

Think about how many clients a coach only offering individual, in-person coaching can support compared to a coach who may work with groups on one day of the week, a team on another, while offering individual coaching services on yet another day of the week. That same coach may also offer an on-demand, video-based program based on needs they were hearing from the groups that they served.

How do you want to spend your time?

_____

_____

What is important for you?

_____

_____

Understanding Our Business Motivations or Drivers

In my own work, I coach, train, speak, offer online courses. I do individual team and group coaching around topics related to leadership, teamwork, and business success. It's very easy for me to say yes to work and sometimes very exciting.

At the same time, I really need to be key or clear about what are my business drivers or motivations:

Is it to **generate revenue?**

Is it to **be challenged in the work** that I do, to meet my own motivational needs?

OR, is it to **provide stretch for myself** as a business owner?

If I fill myself with work that doesn't pay enough, and my driver is pay and revenue at the end of the day, then will I be satisfied when I hit my threshold? Will my requirements and needs be met? Think about what you really want to create.

Questions to think about—

What are the drivers for you in your work?

_____

_____

_____

WHY do you want to run a business?

_____

_____

_____

Write out the top 5 drivers that will motivate you.

_____

_____

_____

What are the activities that will capitalize on your strengths?

_____

_____

_____

Consistency

A third area in business development is about being **consistent**. Now there's a lot that you're probably hearing about what **you need to be doing** as a coach to generate business. You *need to have* a blog, you **need to be** on social media.

If we listen to all the noise that is in the market place, then we may start filling our time with tasks that:

#1—Don't add value

#2—Don't meet the needs of your clients

#3—Don't leverage your strengths

#4—Are so dilute that they don't have an impact.

Unfortunately, I see a lot of people building their business doing something a few times, then stopping it and wondering why it didn't work.

They might blog twice, don't see the results and wonder, "Why didn't I get results?" Consistency is about doing things frequently enough so that we give each one a fair trial.

For more tools on this, check out these resources in Section 5:

1. The Back Pages—Brainstorming Sheet—Use this to brainstorm what you want to talk about.
2. The Content Planner—Annual Overview is provided to help you identify when you want to schedule that calendar.
3. The Monthly Content Tracker can be used to track what goes out when, and what response(s) you have.

Reflection questions:

What are the consistent tasks important to do regularly?

_____

_____

Who can do them?

_____

_____

Who doesn't need to do them?

_____

_____

As we get clear on what we like to do, we can do it consistently over time and again. These consistent actions can capitalize or leverage our strengths as we move forward.

We also want to **track**. We want to be looking at analytics. If you're blogging, what do your analytics say? What are people hungry for? What's not getting much interest? Data in today's corporate arena is king, and as small business owners, we want to look at the data we have at our fingertips.

Use the Monthly Daily Tracker in Section 5 to note your analytics. You might track followers, or newsletter subscribers, or website visits. Consider what data, and frequency, is useful for you.

The Sparker—Jenn's Story

One of the greatest benefits of running a business is that we can really have a lot of control over our business as coaches. If we're doing a lot of virtual work in our coaching business, we can work from almost anywhere. In fact, most of the summer, typically most of July and August, I work out of Muskoka, beautiful, beautiful location, a couple of hours north of Toronto. I work out of a ninety-year-old cottage.

I wake up in the morning, I "dial in" to my clients and groups from the river. I may look out of my office and see a blue heron across the river. These are, in fact, some of my most productive times working out of the cottage and that was part of my vision when I started back in 2004. I wanted to make sure that I would have time to enjoy the few precious weeks that are nice here in Canada in the summer.

So, as you move forward, I want you to think about what you ultimately want to create. With hard work and by making significant choices we can decide what are those points of the year when **we want to move, how we want to operate, and what's important**? And while it may not manifest right away, it is so important to have that strong vision over time.

Not Reinventing the Wheel

Another business fundamental to explore is getting you to think about **not reinventing the wheel**. There is so much that has been road tested at this time. I think it's really important that you develop a network and connect with others **in the** coaching community, as well as connect with others **outside of** the coaching community. Whether you decide to join a local ICF chapter, a group within coach-training schools, really be listening for **what is working, what's the trend, and what's not**. Then think about how it matches your style.

From others, what do you hear about:

What's working?

_____

_____

What are the trends?

_____

_____

What doesn't work?

_____

_____

How does this match your style?

_____

_____

In saying "listen for what's tried and true," some of you may not want to follow the regular beaten path. I personally have really been a bit of a renegade in that when I first started getting trained as a coach, I was still a team leader. I was still a program manager operating within the United Nations system and every month for the span of five to six months, I would travel up to Toronto from where I was based, go through a weekend of coach training, and then bring it back to my team in the Caribbean.

One of my biggest questions as a coach (while still a leader) was, "How do we bring it into teams?". Back then in 2003, I got a lot of resistance from others in the coaching profession. People saying, "Oh, that's training, you know. We don't really do coaching within with groups or with teams."

As many of you know a large focus of my work since 2004 has been to help establish and further the sub-disciplines of group coaching and team coaching along with other thought leaders in the field.

So, think about what's going to work best for you and what is that stamp that you want to be making?

To-Do and Not-To-Do Lists

I've said a couple times already, we want to build on strengths. We can't mitigate every weakness. The research around strengths originally showed that it takes more effort to bring a weakness up than to magnify a strength. As a solopreneur, if skills are important, and they are—don't get me wrong—think finances, admin, these activities need to get done.

One, we can do it all ourselves. If this is the path we choose, think about the training you need. Think about the time it will take.

Two, if you don't want to do it yourself, who are the people that will help you do it?

We want to make sure that we have a plan and we prioritize that plan and keep moving. **What are we putting our attention around? How is each activity generating revenue? How is each task or activity building on what we do?**

Activity:

Make a list of all the tasks you undertake or think you may need to undertake. What impact or value does each one have? Do you want to do it, or get someone else?

Task	Impact/Value	How good am I?	Who should do it?

Use **The Monthly Planner**—To-Dos in the CBB Planner as space to indicate your task list on a monthly basis.

Experimentation

A couple of things to be aware of is really challenging yourself to think about getting out, doing things, and **experimenting**.

I see this in my business all the time. There are so many learning curves that we move through on a regular basis as small business owners. If I don't try things a couple of times, things might not actually take root. I have seen this over the years with very successful programs in the long term. The first or second time I ran it, it just wasn't the big wow bang that I thought there would be. What made them become successful was the experimentation I did and the feedback I received from participants and clients. They really became those long-term sustainable programs.

So again, think about what is going to be a learning curve for you. What are those areas that you think might have some good legs and how much effort are you willing to put in to seeing how it will take root? What are the areas of potential learning here?

What do I want to experiment with?

_____

_____

What am I willing to try, and see how it works?

_____

_____

How will I ask for feedback?

_____

_____

Change and Ongoing Development

As we look out to the landscape in which we operate, it's hard not to notice the ongoing change which exists. Even the profession of coaching is one of the newer professions. Research is now catching up to many of our practices. Ongoing change requires fluidity, an open mind, and a willingness to learn. How do you approach change? What are you doing to keep learning?

The Sparker—Jenn's Story

I spent the better part of my first 15 years of working in very intensive team-based environments. From Algonquin Park's intensive summers spent leading a swim staff, to leading multi-national teams of youth volunteers globally, ongoing change and development was a theme from the early years of my career. Nothing remained the same, and the contexts in which I worked were often undergoing significant change—from dictatorship to democracy, or from communities isolated one day and then being connected to the web the next. Change and adaptation was part of my world.

As a professional, this meant keeping abreast with newer skill sets. Skills I would have never anticipated learning about. In 1996/97 I found myself enrolling for a post-graduate certificate in HR. Certainly two years before, after achieving a Masters, I thought my learning was complete. Not so!

Work as a leader, with my bosses thousands of miles away, required that I take learning into my own hands. Participating as a student in those early days of "distance learning" with colleges and universities, often entailed multiple tries to get online, then hours to download materials or upload chat logs and assignments. The benefit of moving through these moments was the reflective pause required in order to do my work better.

The context today of most of our clients is just as rapidly changing. From changes to how we communicate and interrelate, to how we offer our services. Ongoing development is part of our work. Continual Development was even added to the ICF Standards of Ethical Conduct a few years ago to reflect this point.[5]

What are the skill sets that are going to support your evolution as a coach? What else do you think you want to add?

_____

_____

Who can help you evolve? Think peer, mentors, supervisors, etc.

_____

_____

5 https://coachfederation.org/code-of-ethics. Accessed 5.22.18

The Iceberg—Our Mindsets, Behaviors, and Results

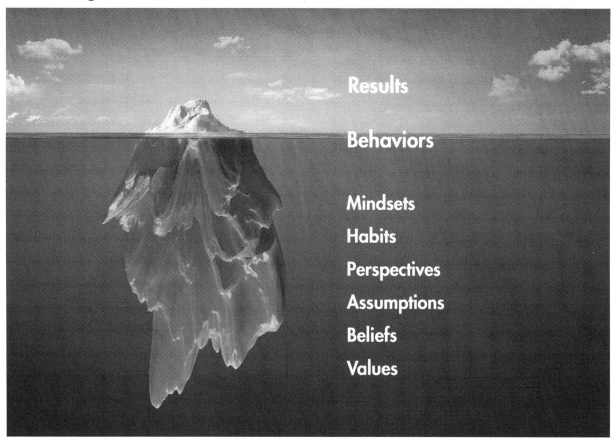

In a business, our results are shaped by many factors. Some of these are visible and are seen through our behaviors. There are also many factors that are "below the water line" of the business, influencing our results.

It's often these items below the water line that are not seen, and we are unconscious to. These are the things that get translated into results and shape our behaviors.

It is these "below the surface" items—values, beliefs, assumptions, perspectives, habits and mindsets—that we explore in the Ecosystem (Section 4) of the workbook.

Our values lead to the behaviors we undertake, which then shape our results. For example, if I value quality, I will spend extra time making sure something is complete and finalized, leading to a product that is complete.

At the deepest level are our **values**, the things we "go to bat" for, and the "lines in the sand" we do not cross. Values shape our decisions, what we prioritize, and also influence the business philosophies for which we take a stand.

I'd like you to think about the values that are driving you in your business right now. What are the things that are important? How are your values around quality or efficiency or customer service or high touch shaping the way you approach your business? Shaping the way you communicate about your business and also shaping the amount of time you put around your business activities?

There can be a lack of alignment between values and behaviors. This is often where we see a lot of disconnect.

When we're able to leverage our values to be true to what is important, we move more into a flow state. As we know with flow, flow allows us to step into our strengths. In flow, there is often challenge involved. Research continues to show that it's at those moments that we are really doing our best work.

What are the key things that are important to you as a business owner? What is the mark that you want to leave?

List your top 5–10 business values in the space provided

If you need a prompt around your values, consider these questions:

- What do you want to be known for?
- What are you going to ensure you do with each product or service you offer?
- When you think of other's products or services, what are you envious of?
- When you think of other's products or services, what gets you angry?

Some of these questions may point to values you hold as a business.

Beyond values, also "below the waterline" are our beliefs, perspectives, assumptions, habits and mindsets. These play an integral role in shaping our actions and decisions.

Carol Dweck's work around Fixed and Growth Mindsets, has brought the discourse about how we see the world, and what we believe, into new spheres–from education to leadership.

Now going hand in hand with values are our **belief systems**. These are often really buried below the waterline. Beliefs are shaped through our socialization, our family, our life experiences also continue to drive how we see and operate within the world.

As a business owner, I might have a belief that entrepreneurial risks are important, in contrast to another business owner. How did I get to those ideas? Well, number one, my father was an entrepreneur. Entrepreneurship is a way to sustain a family. My belief it might also be shaped by working in non-traditional environments where risk was much more common every day. Also, my work experience had me living in countries where the notion of a job for life was not reflected in employment contracts in the country.

In making the business flow, we want to make sure that what is underneath the waterline is lined up with what's above the waterline.

Part of this is also getting to the core of our belief systems.

On the next page, there will be space to identify the beliefs that are driving your behavior as well as the beliefs that are not. Think about what your top five beliefs are. *What are the beliefs that will run or influence your business? What behaviors does it lead to? What results do you get?* Take a few minutes to work through the worksheet.

After you've made this list, take a look back at what you see, and circle the ones that are enabling beliefs, and which ones are hindering or stopping you (also known as derailers).

As coaches, a lot of work is about helping clients shift from limiting beliefs to enabling beliefs. As a coach yourself, what are you able to do to reframe, refocus, retool your belief systems?

We know it's not easy. It may also be connected to some of these other areas, perspectives, assumptions, mindset, and habits.

As business owners, we bring a variety of **perspectives** about ourselves, our staff members, our stakeholders. These are influenced by context, by socialization, by what we do and how we relate with the world. Think about the perspectives you hold, and what behaviors they lead to.

What results come out of the perspectives you are standing in?

Work around perspectives is a significant area in our work as coaches. When you're coaching a client who says, "I'm really stuck in business right now." I might ask them, "What perspective are you holding around that?".

They might reply, "The perspective is that it's so hard that I feel like I'm climbing up a mountain."

My response might be, "If you find that you're climbing up a mountain, what are some alternative perspectives that you could be embracing to help you move from A to B?"

They may reframe their perspective to "While I am climbing the mountain I also realize that I have a team with me, excellent Sherpas and I've prepared for months to do this."

This perspective will lead to a series of very different results than the first perspective of "It feels like I am climbing the mountain."

Deep below the waterline is also the notion of **assumptions**. Henry Winkler wrote that, "assumptions are the termites of relationships."[6] I would assert that assumptions are the termites of any business.

It is really important that we take time to unpack, name, and identify the assumptions that we're making as a coaching business. I recognize that one of the assumptions I make every day is that people will want to join me virtually. I assume that people are perhaps frustrated with time and effort spent in travel, so they will prefer to join me virtually. That has given me confidence to offer most of my work virtually, and not in-person.

Think through the assumptions that you're making in your business and the behaviors that they lead to. What results do you get from the assumptions you make?

A final area just above the waterline related to behaviors are **habits**. Habits are things that we do consistently and often subconsciously. Habits become automatic ways of doing things, often without much thought. Habits can be in service to our work, and also can get in the way of our success.

---

6 https://www.brainyquote.com/quotes/henry_winkler_320340

Think about these habits:

- Getting into the office early to get high focus work complete before your calls start
- "Switching off" and not undertaking any social media over the weekend
- Ensuring financial payments are addressed as soon as they are received
- Attending a conference or event every year
- Replying to emails right away
- Filing emails right away to always keep your inbox at zero

As you think about habits, what is the reason? Why are you habitually doing these things? What results are the habits giving you? Which ones are helping you? Which ones are hindering you?

Worksheet instructions:

Take a few minutes filling out the worksheet on the different values, beliefs, perspectives, assumptions, habits, and mind-sets that drive your business.

Worksheet—Explore What's Below the Waterline of your Business

Use this to identify:

Values	What behaviors does it lead to?	What results does it lead to?
Quality	Always reviewing a document a second time before it is sent. Regular evaluations and feedback on work.	Offering products that are aligned with what clients really need. Making changes as needed.

Beliefs	What behaviors does it lead to?	What results does it lead to?
"I Can"	Persistence, Risk Taking, Innovation.	Pushing through barriers. More experimentation.

Perspectives	What behaviors does it lead to?	What results does it lead to?
"Waterfall"	Trusting that the flow will be there.	Focusing on passive revenue projects in the "downtime" so the flow will be there. Taking breaks to recharge when things are slower.

Assumptions	What behaviors does it lead to?	What results does it lead to?
"I need to charge less in order to sell more."	Charging below market rate.	Only a 5% bump in sales which does not translate to the sales increase.

Habits	What behaviors does it lead to?	What results does it lead to?
Getting into the office at 6 am.	One hour of focused project work, uninterrupted.	Better design, more detail, more creative projects. Getting things done more quickly.

Mindsets	What behaviors does it lead to?	What results does it lead to?
Optimist	Continuing to try even when things aren't going well. Believing that things will be better tomorrow.	More experimentation. Consistent actions through the ups and downs.

Your Vision:

Seneca once wrote:

"If a man knows not to which port he sails, no wind is favorable."[7]

Our vision is something that pulls us forward through the choppy, and sometimes turbulent, waters of business and life. Vision is aspirational, calling us forward, as well as moving us through the ups and downs. One of the activities in the next section is a collection of 20+ questions for you to work through. Please take a moment and flip to page 95 to complete that exercise right now.

Business Fundamentals

Cash Flow is King

At the end of the day as businesses, we are here to generate money. There needs to be adequate resources coming in the door. We often say cash flow is king. If not, we're operating at a deficit. Depending on the resources we have around us, deficit can ultimately lead to business decline or close.

What are your minimum financial requirements every month? What about every quarter? Every year?

_____

_____

_____

What are your business revenues? What will draw in revenue for you? Refer to the Funnel—What's on offer?

_____

_____

_____

7 https://www.goodreads.com/quotes/76815-if-a-man-knows-not-to-which-port-he-sails

When do you think people will access different services? What implications will this have for cash flow?

_____

_____

_____

With these responses in mind, how many clients would you need to serve? Use the following to do some projections about different options for the mix of your client work.

	Option A	Option B	Option C
Individual Clients			
Group Clients			
Team Clients			
Book sales or product sales			
Other			

The One-Percent Rule to Business Development

Businesses can be built in sprints–whether that happens over weeks, months or years. The world of "agile" is teaching us about the importance of "rapid iteration," experimentation and speeding things up. In my own business, some of the programs that used to run for a day, are now compressed to a few hours of deep focus.

The One-Percent Rule to business development gets you thinking about taking small steps every day. Over time, these steps add up. Consider some of your major goals right now, what would a 1% increment look like in each of these goals?

Overall, the business development cycle is iterative and consists of several different stages including:

Create/refine the vision

Prepare

Create an action plan

Seek out support

Take ongoing small steps

Test, Retest, Learn

Learn, Iterate, Act

Achieve goals

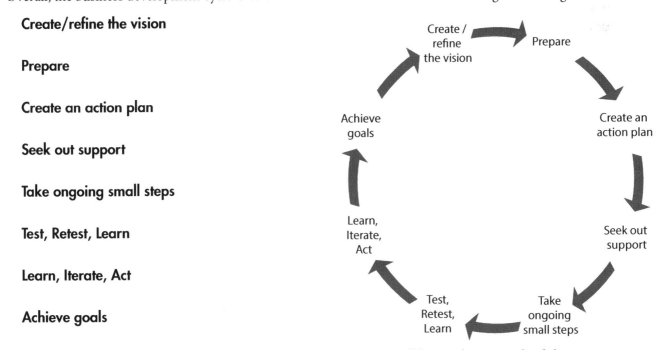

Throughout the manual, particularly the Ecosystem section, we'll be exploring each of these areas.

Bonus Resource:

For those that enjoy the space of reflective practice, I have available "28 Days of Journaling Prompts" as a bonus. These can be downloaded at https://www.CoachingBusinessBuilder.com.

Core Business Fundamentals Metaview

Before we wrap up this section, I'd like you to think about these core business fundamentals for you as a business owner. In coaching we use the term "metaview" to refer to the 30,000 foot view of your business.

Think about the things you want to do, as well as the things you don't want to do in your business. That's going to look very different for each one of us.

Write down what's on your to-do list and not-to-do list. Maybe it's related to some of these tips that you've seen in this first section. Maybe it's something else. Take a few minutes to think about these things. Enjoy!

Things I want to do	Things I don't want to do but need to, to run the business

Once you have completed your list, ask yourself:

What tasks can be delegated? Deferred? Done by others? Deleted? Circle or mark these in your table.

End-of-Section Checkpoint

What are the key items you want to remember from this section?

_____

_____

What do you want to add to your plans?

_____

_____

What has become really clear for you so far?

_____

_____

Section 2
Solopreneur Primer

This section is called the Solopreneur Primer and evolved out of my 12th anniversary celebrations back in 2016 when I highlighted 12 Essential Business Lessons, one for each year of business. Just as the word *primer* indicates, these tips are bite-size pieces that I hope will get you going. It's not intended to replace much deeper work.

What's a primer? To set the stage, here's a quick definition. First, a primer is anything that is used for priming. The Merriam-Webster dictionary refers to it as "a substance used as a preparatory coat on previously unpainted wood, metal, or canvas, especially to prevent the absorption of subsequent layers of paint or the development of rust."

In this instance, it refers to a base coat so everything else can stick to it. What is the primer of your business? How are you creating a foundation so other things—hopefully business revenue—can stick to it?

Second, they define it as "a cap or cylinder containing a compound which responds to friction or an electrical impulse and ignites the charge in a cartridge or explosive." Here a primer can be a compound **used to ignite** an explosive charge. I love this because as business owners, we are looking for that ignition switch. We're looking to see what will catalyze us, spark us, boost us and get us going.

Now, Merriam-Webster also has a third definition of primer: "a small pump for pumping fuel to prime an internal combustion engine, especially in an aircraft." In priming a pump or an engine, we need that to get going. In this light, I hope that these ideas are useful for you. Maybe this fits you more.

Certainly, as someone who has done a lot of painting in my lifetime I can guarantee that priming is hard work and is an essential part of a successful end. Some of you may not know this, but in my early years in working in international development, I was based at the community level. I've helped build schools around the world and part of that involved getting out onto construction sites. Priming is key if you've ever worked with wood. The quality and the cleanliness of the wood is key in ensuring that you've got a good base for a coat. I hope that you'll also think about this as priming you to get ready for business or get ready for that next jump in your business.

What foundation is important for you to prime or get ready?

_____

_____

Some of you may know that I'm a scientist by training. Originally, I completed an undergrad science degree in psychology at McGill University. As such, I often look to the scientific practice. Merriam-Webster also includes the definition of a primer as "a molecule, as a short strand of RNA or DNA, whose presence is required for the formation of another molecule such as a longer chain of DNA."

With this final definition, we're really seeing that, in fact, primers require other things to do their job. That that is part of the intent of this book—to support you so you can do your job. In working through the different sections I hope that you will get a better idea of what priming means for you.

Take a moment to note what PRIMER means for you in your business right now.

_____

_____

_____

One of the key things that's been important for me in my work is to continue enhancing the dialogue amongst the coaching community and the small business world. I hope that as you go through this course, it will spark some new ideas as well as create new conversations between you and your peers.

As we get going, I'd like you to consider a couple of questions:

I'd like you to imagine yourself and your business twelve years from now.

What could your business look like?

_____

_____

What are you doing?

_____

_____

Who are you working with?

_____

_____

What's happening?

_____

_____

What are the key things that are moving you from A to B?

_____

_____

When I opened the doors to Potentials Realized in 2004, metaphorically of course, I knew that I really wanted to continue to impact people all over the world. And you'll read, I've been able to do that in a virtual business.

I have just stepped into my 15th year of business. I really wanted to distill down some of the things that combined have allowed the business and my work to ignite. Ignite not only the people that I work with, but those who have helped me grow Potentials Realized.

This section is geared for Solopreneurs. A solopreneur is defined as "a person who gets up and runs a business of their own." Are you a solopreneur?

For me, it's been an intentional business decision to continue to run a business that is *lean and mean, or small, scalable, and agile.* As needed, I bring in people who can help me out, who partner with me as we roll out larger initiatives. I've chosen in this phase of my work to do it myself. As the business owner and founder, it comes down to me at the end of the day, which can be very exciting.

It can also be very scary at times. There can be a lot of responsibility. As someone who led global teams for more than a decade where I was responsible for hundreds of people in more extreme work environments I know what it's like to shoulder responsibility and concern. I also know that following your passions is worth facing fear head on.

Since 2004, in phase two of my career, I have wanted to create a business that was really driven by my passions and shaped by the lifestyle I wanted to create. These two items are driving forces for many solopreneurs—**passion and lifestyle.**

What's important for you as you grow your work?

_____

_____

What are the passions you want to incorporate into your work?

_____

_____

What's the lifestyle you want to create?

_____

_____

Vision

In our work as coaches, supporting clients to create a compelling and exciting vision is often one of our starting points. As a solopreneur or business owner, this also is a critical step. Having an exciting vision pulls us through the ebbs and flows of business—the ups and downs.

As a starting point, I wanted to provide you with an opportunity to reconnect with your vision as a solopreneur. You may choose to work through the questions provided in the book OR you may want to go and gather up some of your own vision materials–photographs, trinkets, and other artifacts to represent where you are going.

As I recently wrote, visions help to clarify. They also help to pull us forward through the ups and downs, and the ebbs and flows, that are inevitable in a business and I would say the ups and downs continue along the way. They don't just go away after your first year of business. Vision constantly evolves and, hopefully, remains as a touchpoint for us at all stages.

Page 95 goes through some vision questions you can walk through systematically, use the following space to capture words, ideas, and images of your business vision:

Use the following space to write out, and capture, elements of your vision.

_____

_____

_____

_____

_____

_____

_____

_____

_____

Be True to Who You Are

"Think big and don't listen to people who tell you it can't be done. Life's too short to think small." –Tim Ferris[8]

Solopreneur Tip #2 is being true to who you are. As business owners, we're constantly being challenged. We are challenged by our customers, our clients, and we are challenged by ourselves. As business owners, there can be a lot of doubt in terms of what we do. Therefore, it's important to be clear about who we are and be true to who we are.

I think it's very rare to find a successful business owner who has not been true to themselves, true to their skills, talents, abilities, and, of course, their passions. So, in this module we're going to be looking at what's important to you.

Reflect on these questions:

Why are you developing this business? *Is it to make a lot of money? And that's OK. Again, as business owners, we want to make money. Is it to make a mark on the world? Is it to impact more people?*

_____

_____

What's important for you in starting a business, especially starting a solopreneur business? *As independent business owners, we may feel like we are driving the bus. If the bus breaks down, we want to make sure that we have someone we can call on or be able to fix it ourselves.*

_____

_____

_____

8 http://www.azquotes.com/quote/554762

What is it that you want to create? *I'm recognizing it might not be something you create immediately in the first year, but, ultimately, what kind of business do you want to create?*

_____

_____

What is it that you want to offer? *What are the things you want to have on offer to your clients and who are they?*

_____

_____

The Sparker—Jenn's Story

Like many entrepreneurs my pathway into business ownership was not a straight line. Back in 2003, I lost some vision permanently in one eye due to an eye infection. Literally overnight my career changed course. I knew that I was not going to be able to continue to move around the world as I had. The future was very uncertain.

After months of soul-searching, I realized that it was time to return to Canada after being abroad for more than a decade. I also knew that I wanted to continue working around team and people development issues. I decided to turn my attention to founding and building Potentials Realized. I had no idea how this would happen, but I knew it would be important to continue to reach out and work with people all over the globe. Keep in mind it was 2004, and while there was the internet, but we really didn't have the same technology we have today. The iPad and tablets had not yet come onto the scene. Skype was just emerging, and we certainly didn't have zoom. I am so thankful that technology has continued to change and has allowed me to continue innovating and connecting with people all over the world.

So, think about you. What kind of business do you want to create? What is it that you want to offer? Who do you want to work with? What do you want to have on offer for them? I think it's also important for us to think about what we want our work to look like. As I meet my clients in large organizations, small organizations, government services, many of them are envious about the fact that for two months of every year I get to work in beautiful Muskoka, Canada. I have a tiny office in a small cabin in the woods. It's been in our family for generations and while it's very basic, there is nothing more precious than being able to walk outside in the morning as the sun is coming up over the hills and hitting the lake and just being there in silence and solitude of nature.

As I started building my business I knew it would be so important in my work to have creative renewal time "up north" in Muskoka, but I was not sure how it would work. I held onto the vision of making it happen and enjoy my ultra-productive summer work schedule, without a lot of the usual distractions

Building a business can be hard work. It's taken sacrifice to create a business that works for me and more for my family. The fact that I was the primary, and only, bread earner in my family for several years I think was the "spark" to keep me trying and innovating.

Be True to Who You Are—The Micro-Vision

It can be useful to create a micro-vision for what your every day work looks like. Take a few minutes to reflect on the following questions to think about what you want a typical day, week, or month to look like. Sometimes we are working around the clock or every day when projects are full stream, so what do you want your work to look like?

What do you want your work to look like? Think of a typical week, day or month.

_____

_____

Now come up with five or ten words that really represent what's important to you as a business owner, what's important to you as a solopreneur. Think about how you want your business to reflect you. What are those things you will go to bat for?

Take a few minutes to identify five to ten things that are important to you in your business. Maybe it is about having flexibility. Maybe it is about being able to work from anywhere. Maybe it's about taking certain months of the year off.

1. _____

2. _____

3. _____

4. _____

5. _____

6. _____

7. _____

8. _____

9. _____

10. _____

Our visions can also shift over time. Six months into my business, I was working out of the place I thought I wanted to be—Muskoka—until the snow started flying. That's when I realized it was time to move back to Toronto for the winter. It shifted my vision a bit. But every year I've been able to get up there, not always for two months each summer, but certainly for significant blocks of time.

 Checkpoint: Reflect back to Section 1, is there anything you want to add, or change to your vision, based on these activities? When do you want to revisit it?

Strengths and Flow

The third primer tip is all about strengths. As I have shared, I've chosen to keep my business lean and mean. It's been a conscious decision. I often get asked every year, *"Aren't you going to bring on more people? Aren't you going to grow this business?"* Well, I spent many years leading global teams. I still work with teams. Yet, I love being a bit of a lone wolf. As a wolf, we are still part of a pack, but we can also be a lone wolf at times.

As solopreneurs, we want to get clear on what our strengths are. It's really important along the way to leverage our strengths. As coaches we may be undertaking this work with our clients. Gallup has found that people who leverage their strengths are **six times more engaged** and report a **three-times-higher quality of life**[9].

There are so many reasons why strengths are important. Of course, there's always a flip side. Countering our strengths are our weaknesses. I don't think weaknesses are a focus for many of us who work with strengths. While I think it's important to always leverage our strengths, we also want to watch for the blind spots. If we're always using our strengths, we may create blind spots we're not aware of.

A useful framework that I've used for decades now in my cross-cultural work is termed the Johari window. Many of you might be familiar with the Johari window which evolved from the work of two social psychologists Joseph Luft and Harrington Ingham. The premise starts with the importance of opening the windows to our knowledge of ourselves.

There are things that we know that we keep hidden, as well as things that others and ourselves know. There's also a space here where others know things that we don't know—or things that are blind spots. Finally, there are things that we don't know, and others don't know. Perhaps there are sides to us that have never been tapped because we have never needed to explore them.

The notion of the Johari Window is that we want to open all the windows equally, particularly when we need to work interdependently and in partnership with others.

My guess is that during your journey as a solopreneur some of *those blind* areas might become more visible, and could get in the way, and you might find that the things you have kept hidden come out to the light. The hidden weaknesses can be mitigated by partnerships.

We might be great at things. As solopreneurs, we want to recognize that we're not over-utilizing our strengths as these can become blind spots. Under times of pressure and stress, we may naturally revert and lean into these strengths, over magnifying them. It is useful to have trusted advisors around to share with us when we are not reaching our full potential.

---

9 http://news.gallup.com/businessjournal/186044/employees-strengths-outperform-don.aspx (accessed 4.22.18)

Take a few minutes to complete your own Johari Window:

Open (Known to self and others)	**Blind** (Not known to self but known to others)
Hidden (Known to self but not to others)	**Unknown** (Not known to self or others)

As coaches, it is likely that we have already worked with a variety of strengths tools with our clients. The first part of optimizing strengths is to first identify your strengths.

There are a wide variety of strengths-based assessments available:

- StrengthsFinder from Gallup
- VIA Strengths from the positive psychology movement
- Strengths Deployment Inventory
- From the team coaching realm—the Team Diagnostic from Team Coaching International

If you have taken any of these, now is a great time to pull them out again and take a look.

Another way to identify your strengths is to ask those around you. You might ask others:

- What do you see as my strengths?
- What do you notice in my work?
- How would you describe my strengths?
- What are the three adjectives you would use to describe my strengths.

It is important to identify strengths, whether we're doing it for ourselves or doing it with clients. In many coaching models or coaching processes, we have an approach of using adjectives to identify strengths. I'll often say, "*What are the three adjectives that describe your brand or business owner?*" Or I'll ask my clients, based on the work that we've done, "*What are the three adjectives you'd use to describe our work together?*"

Over time we can learn, we can listen, we can hear, what people see in terms of our brand, and our strengths as business owners. As solopreneurs, I think it's important to not only identify and learn, but we want to build onto our strengths. We want to build these into our plan. We want to build it into our goals and use those strengths on a regular basis.

Activity:

As solopreneurs it is important to be able to leverage our strengths given that we are usually the one we rely on. Your activity for this lesson is to get you thinking about your strengths.

What are your strengths?

_____

_____

What three adjectives would others use to describe you?

_____

_____

_____

How are you using them? What examples do you have of your strengths in action?

_____

_____

_____

What projects or tasks are leveraging your strengths?

_____

_____

Which projects aren't using your strengths? Who can help you with this?

_____

_____

How, and when, are you overusing your strengths?

_____

_____

_____

How are your strengths becoming a blind spot for you?

_____

_____

_____

What changes do you want to make?

_____

_____

Use the following chart to summarize what you have listed:

Strength	Blind spot	Change/Modification

What do you notice?

If you haven't undertaken a strengths-based assessment in a while, maybe do another one. See how it's changed or remained the same.

I did VIA Strengths as I opened the doors here at Potentials Realized in 2004 and at that time one of my top strengths was *bravery*. I think that was representative of who I was and what I took a stand for in the world every day in my former world of work. My work was on the edge: on the edge of poverty alleviation, on the edge of helping communities rebuild after natural disasters; bravery was certainly important in the world of work that I used to rotate in.

Recently I redid my VIA Strengths and *bravery* dropped off the list. What showed up, though, was more around relationships. A key part of my success has been about building relationships, one conversation at a time. And, of course, *love of learning* was still at the top of my list. I've been very fortunate to intentionally create a business that represents my experience. I'm an educator at heart. I love working with people, sparking conversation, and bringing people together.

I hope that this short story was an effective illustration to get you thinking about your favorite moments that you've had, where you are at your best, and how some of your strengths flow out of those situations. Before moving on, be sure to work through this strengths activity.

Flow

As an undergrad psychology student in the early 1990s, I remember one of my favorite course assignments was to read *Flow* by Mihaly Csikszentmihalyi. The book had just been released. I was doing a third-year course on Learning. It was amazing! I was captivated by this idea of "flow" already in my early twenties and could see moments of FLOW in my athleticism as a swimmer and a competitive rower. I truly recognized when I was in "flow" as a student when I found myself at that place where my skills were being challenged, but just with enough stretch to really lose myself in the moment. The concept of flow has carried throughout my entire world of work.

"The best moments in our lives are not the passive, receptive, relaxing times… The best moments usually occur if a person's body or mind is stretched to its limits in a voluntary effort to accomplish something difficult and worthwhile."
–Mihaly Csikszentmihalyi[10]

Designing a world of work that has incorporated flow has been integral to each part of my career. I still like to ensure that every day is filled with challenge and learning. With my international work throughout the 90s I would wake up and ask myself, *"Are people really paying me to do this?"* It was amazing. I got to live in the Caribbean for more than a decade. I worked with phenomenal people who, yes, were facing amazing challenges but also had such resilience and flow.

Reflection Questions:

When do you find that moments of flow occur for you?

_____

_____

What does that signal about what you are good at and where your stretch is?

_____

_____

Journaling Activity:

Think about a time when you were "at your best." Write about that experience. What were the strengths you were able to use and lean into?

_____

_____

 Checkpoint: What do you want to add to, or tweak, about your vision? You may want to translate some of the vision items to specific action steps using the One Page Plan found in Section 5. Is there anything you want to add to your action plan/One Page Plan around your strengths and flow?

Don't Just Do It Once (Mastery, Repurpose, and Republish)

Lesson #4 I've entitled "Don't Just Do It Once." Don't just do it once. Think about your efforts so far. Whether you've been in business for one day or 1,000 days, how many times have you just let a project, task, or program go at one time.

I would like you to think about where repetition can create power. Malcolm Gladwell wrote in his book, *Outliers*, that it takes 10,000 hours to create mastery. In recent years there have been numerous studies regarding the concept of mastery. This has been a long-standing question and has been researched by many in addition to Malcolm Gladwell. Ericsson's 1993 research first explored this concept of Deliberative Practice. He indicates that it involves, "stepping outside your comfort zone and trying activities beyond your current abilities."[11]

---

10 Mihaly Csikszentmihalyi, Flow, 1990, p. 3
11 http://www.businessinsider.com/anders-ericsson-how-to-become-an-expert-at-anything-2016-6

Some recent studies have said that only 12% of performance variance can be attributed to practice[12]. There are other things key to this is in our work. How many times does it take to really make a product excellent? How many times does it take to reach a deep level of practice?

There are several elements that must be present in order to really learn and master skills. There needs to be a mindfulness. Just doing something without the reflection is not engaging in that deeper level of learning or what is called *deep practice*. Deep practice involves three steps:

1. There needs to be some struggle.
2. Repeat it.
3. Feel it.

Resource: Deep Practice, Daniel Coyle, The Talent Code

Think of those things that recently you have learned from. How have these three elements been present?

I have said for years, "If things were easy, we wouldn't really be learning." I look at my own history where most of the learning has been uncomfortable.

The Sparker—Jenn's Story

Matthew, my son, is a tennis player. He's seeing how practice really does make perfect and sometimes we must work. We must move through those difficult steps to become more effective.

It's been a pleasure to see him grow as a tennis player. Tennis was always a sport that I enjoyed. I wasn't as good as he has gotten. I still get a chance to play with him, but because of partial vision in one eye I'm never going to be good at eye-hand coordination. I just don't have the necessary depth perception anymore.

In learning skills, repetition is key. When I drop Matthew off on Saturday afternoons to tennis practice, I go to the library to work. When I come back it always amazes me how much progress he's made in only two hours. Time and practice helps us improve.

In business, I'd like you to think about repetition. What does this mean for your business?

_____

_____

Make a list of things you repeat on a regular basis. Think projects, tasks, client support, etc.

_____

_____

12 https://www.psychologicalscience.org/news/releases/becoming-an-expert-takes-more-than-practice.html, accessed 5.1.18

Which of these tasks have become easier over time?

_____

_____

Where have you developed mastery?

_____

_____

Where do you need to develop more mastery? What would that take?

_____

_____

There's a high element of trust that's connected to this. As Steve Jobs wrote,

"You can't connect the dots looking forward; you can only connect them looking backward. So you have to trust that the dots will somehow connect in your future. You have to trust in something—your gut, destiny, life, karma, whatever. This approach has never let me down, and it has made all the difference in my life." [13]

The Sparker—Jenn's Story

There have been many times over the history of Potentials Realized where I have wanted to, and even sometimes decided to, throw in the towel on things. There was a moment back in 2008 during our third year of offering the Group Coaching Essentials program that I began to question if this was going to be a program that truly provided value for coaches. In fact, this was just before my first book deal was signed.

I knew there was value, but at the time I wasn't sure it was something I wanted to put attention around. I was getting very involved in many larger corporate projects involving program design and leadership development work. And I wondered if I was right in continuing to offer a program if it wasn't going to be an immediate revenue generator.

Flash forward to today–Year 13 of the program. I've had hundreds of coaches go through the program, influencing conversations all over the world. My books are used by coach training schools globally. I am so glad that I did continue to offer the Group Coaching Essentials program! It's important to recognize that sometimes we just need to keep going a little bit further before things really take root and create their own traction and momentum.

So, in terms of the power of repetition, this lesson is all about not just doing things once. It is an encouragement for you to really think about what you have in your arsenal already. Maybe it's things that you've done.

---

13 https://www.brainyquote.com/quotes/steve_jobs_416875

Repurpose

The second part of this tip is think about what you can **repurpose**. Think about activities you've undertaken. What would you want to do again? And what changes would you make? The path to mastery, whether it's 10,000 hours or whether it's 12%, is not focused on how long it takes us to get there, but on how we learn and grow as solopreneurs.

Every time we do things we learn. Sometimes we can be doing ourselves a disservice by throwing in the towel too early and sometimes it's the best thing to do. Sometimes it's best to repurpose items we've already started. In fact, this workbook and planner has its' roots in several earlier products I launched. The Solopreneur Primer was originally published as an on-demand course over at my Teachable site, and the Inner Biz Leader section grows out of some of the business planning virtual retreat work I've done for the last decade. Years of discussions and presentations with small business owners also have shaped this workbook and planner.

As in any business, with business relationships and business activities, we don't have a crystal ball. Given that so much can change, it's important to be true to ourselves, true to what we want to create. It's also important to look at our strengths which will help us make decisions in terms of:

- how much is enough?
- how many times is enough?
- where do we want to put our attention?

So, as you reflect on these questions, I hope that you will also go back to your evolving business vision for 12 years, 10 years, or even just the next year. Think about what it means to do things more than once for you in the work that you're doing. Use the Vision Questions found in Section 4, page 95.

Republish

The final category here is republish. Today's social media world is so full that just publishing something once is like doing something once and walking away. What can you do to republish, or re-syndicate your content so that it is seen by a wider audience?

Consider:

- Can a blog post become a newsletter article?
- Can something you post on Facebook, also get posted on Instagram or Twitter?
- Can what you said as a guest speaker for a podcast become the roots of a new program?
- Can your online program become a book (just like this section on the solopreneur primer did here as this Section)?

Activity:

Make a list of the core content you have. Where is it currently found or what shape is it in? How might it be repurposed or republished?

_____

_____

_____

_____

_____

Looking ahead to new content creation:

Take 15 minutes to brainstorm or Mind Map your ideas for content you'd like to create. You may want to use the Content Brainstorm Sheet in the Planner Section.

Think about:

- The themes
- The actual articles or blog posts you could write on
- When are you going to schedule these? Is there a monthly or quarterly theme you want to focus on?
- Where would you post them?
- How frequently would you post them?

Connection to the CBB Planner Tools—Section 5

Because content creation can be such a big part of the marketing approach for business owners, refer to these Section 5 tools:

- Use the Back Pages to capture your ideas
- Pick a monthly theme
- Use the Content Calendar to schedule these
- Use the Monthly Content Trackers to track the posts you have made, visits received and notes about the posts
- Use the One Line a Day each day of the month to make notes about your content, or your business in general
- Use the Content Collaboration worksheet to identify partners who can help you expand the reach of your content. Use the bottom part of the page to identify content you can repurpose and republish
- Write these into your Daily Planner Sheets. Copies can be downloaded at CoachingBusinessBuilder.com.

Collaboration

Part 5 of this section is all about collaboration and partnering. As solopreneurs, it's important that we leverage the expertise of people around us. In stepping into these partnerships it's important that we know our strengths, it's important that we know what we're good at and what areas we could benefit from support.

As coaches, we may be collaborating on multiple levels for partnering and collaboration. We may be collaborating when we:

- Partner with other coaches to co-facilitate a program
- Partner with our clients
- Collaborate with others to deliver a multi-dimensional program, for example, being a coach attached to a larger leadership-development initiative
- Partnering with service providers who can help to round out our business–for example, accountants or graphic designers

The word "collaborate" comes from the Latin root of **collaborare,** which means "to labor together." Hopefully it's fun labor. Again, one of the stakes I have in my work is that I really want to make it fun. Now, I don't know about you, but I had to take Latin as a high school student. I don't think they require it anymore. This was many, many moons ago, but it really did serve a great purpose in my life. This skill has certainly has supported me as a writer.

Think about the scope of the work that you want to undertake and who can help you get there as a solopreneur. There are a number of areas that we can be collaborating within around program offerings, program design, and bringing on subcontractors. We can still be a one-person show by bringing on a virtual team around us. Whether we want support in accounting, graphic design, or even if we need an assistant, we can find support virtually to maximize the growth of our businesses.

I collaborate with other people, coaches, trainers, and facilitators **to maximize** my work. I think that's an important component of what collaboration offers us as solopreneurs. It offers us an opportunity to expand our impact. It may offer an opportunity to gain expertise or gain experience in other sectors.

Resources:

There are several resources around collaboration I want to point you to because this is a significant area for solopreneurs, and an area I receive a lot of questions around.

I've done quite a bit of writing and speaking on the topic of collaboration over the last few years. In November of 2015, I was a guest speaker at the ICF team and Group Coaching community of practice. and my presentation was on collaboration. You can view it at: https://www.youtube.com/watch?v=GuIjt5Z2b7s

Going back to 2009, with the publication of my first book *Effective Group Coaching,* I felt that it was really important that we start talking about how to create masterful collaboration. The book was starting to get so large that I was asked to pull out the chapter on collaboration. I felt that it was so important that it became a digital chapter on Co-Facilitation, which you can download at: https://www.from12many.com/downloads.html (use code 4411 when prompted). While you are there, be sure to check out the related case studies on group and team coaching, as well as marketing group and team coaching.

That digital chapter then evolved into "Chapter 11—Who Has Your Back?" in my second book, *From One to Many: Best Practices of Team and Group Coaching.* You can pick up a copy at Amazon.

This topic connects in with writing around relationship management and partnering. Resources you may want to check out include:

Keith Ferrazzi—*Who's Got Your Back?*

Michael J. Gelb—*The Art of Connection: 7 Relationship-Building Skills Every Leader Needs Now*

| If you haven't checked out the Top 20 List Activity in the CBB Section do that now. Also consider who you want to collaborate with regarding content by using the Content Collaboration Planner in Section 5 |

Activity:

Think about collaboration and what it means for you.

When and where would it be useful for you to collaborate? On which projects? Make a list here:

_____

_____

Who would you like to collaborate with?

_____

_____

What's important to you about this?

_____

_____

Ingredients for Collaboration:

Let's look at the ingredients for collaboration, what we know about collaboration and what makes it work. Three essential ingredients we are going to explore here are purpose, complimentary skills, and feedback.

Number One—The Purpose:

The purpose of collaboration or WHY we are doing it is key to successful collaboration.

Are we both clear on the purpose? Is there a shared purpose as to why we're collaborating? Remember that collaboration is not always the best approach. Collaboration can take more time, and Morten Hansen, author of *Collaboration*, indicates that "bad collaboration is worse than no collaboration."[14]

It's also important to recognize when collaboration is going to benefit the project and when it may get in the way.

What is the purpose of collaborating?

_____

_____

When will collaboration benefit you?

_____

_____

When will collaboration not be a good strategy?

_____

_____

I want to share a couple of examples of where collaboration was very important and really helped to maximize my impact, improve my products and the services that I offer to my clients. The first area where I regularly collaborate is in team coaching. Co-leading team coaching sessions brings two sets of eyes, voices, and perspectives to team clients. Second, I collaborate with others on special projects. Partnering with experts in other areas expedites projects and magnifies results.

_____

14 Hansen, Moreten. **Collaboration**, Harvard Business Review, 2009.

In my own experience, the most important foundation for successful partnership is that we have compatible values. Values can mean different things—and when we say that work is excellent or masterful we want to make sure that it really, really is. Values can be very subjective. So how do we define them? Through behaviors and adjectives. If values are not aligned, then there can be a disconnect in collaboration and the collaboration may not work. As coaches, you will want to have discussions with partners (potential and firm) about each other's values. You will want to focus on what values mean for you individually and collectively.

What values are important for you in your work and partnerships? What do these values look like behaviorally?

_____

_____

Number Two—Complimentary Skills

What we also know from research, is that great partnerships and great collaborative experiences are usually grounded in complimentary skills. We bring even more to the table when we partner with people who are very different. We may bring a different style. We may bring a different toolbox. This is in service to the clients we serve.

Thinking about your different partnerships and collaboration opportunities, what are the complimentary skills you bring?

Make a list of the different complimentary skills you bring with your partner. What else do you need?

My skills	Partner's skills	Overlap	What else we need

Number Three—Feedback

Now, a final criterion that is important to consider in partnering is feedback. How are you maximizing a feedback loop? How are you sharing things that are working and things that aren't? Feedback is critical, and it is important to keep iterating and changing and adapting as needed. Just because collaboration used to work doesn't mean it will work today. It requires constant attention.

What checkpoints will you build to ensure that you are regularly providing feedback and iterating from there?

_____

_____

With that, I really hope that you've enjoyed this mini lesson on collaboration. Again, I've included it here because I would not be here today if it were not for many great partners that I get to work with.

Who do you want to collaborate with around and on what projects?

What's going to make it rock?

What's going to really make it work?

I've got a lot more queued up for you. Onto the next tip!

Get Out There

Solopreneur Primer Tip six is **get out there**. It's really a short one. One of the key lessons I've learned in business is the importance of continuing to get out there, continuing to build relationships. It's about getting out there and stretching yourself and doing things that maybe initially aren't as comfortable. It's about getting out there to let people know what you have to offer so you can be of service to them.

As practitioners, we have skills that will atrophy, or wither, if we don't use them. I often say coaching is like a muscle. If we don't use it, we're going to lose it. Getting out there is part of our craft. Getting out there and building relationships is also essential in today's business world.

Now getting out there doesn't always mean we're physically getting out there. As many of you know, I spend a large part of my time working virtually. One of the things that I love about our work, which keeps me on my toes and doing my best work **is** the ability to work virtually. Unlike most of my neighbours who can spend two or more hours a day commuting to the city, I walk into my office and plug in. That extra time not spent commuting 2-3 hours each day allows me to get out regularly in my community to swim and socialize, spend more time with my family, and fit in creative projects like this on a regular basis.

So, in saying **get out there**, I want you to think about what getting out there means for you.

> *Building relationships, taking action, sharing what you have to offer is so key in our work. It is about getting out there. What can this look like in your work?*

_____

_____

There is a fallacy that can exist in a business—the fallacy or trap of being perfect. I continue to meet coaches along the way who just feel that they "aren't ready" to get out there. They may not be perfect, or their website isn't complete. You know, in business today, we really don't have time to wait for a lot of things to be perfect.

Now there is a difference between taking something out into the marketplace when it really is not ready versus taking something out that is **good enough** and while it may not be perfect, it's ok. In a good enough mindset, we're constantly iterating and reiterating and that's a business philosophy. There may never be "perfect" given that the context changes so much.

"The world is changing very fast. Big will not beat small anymore. It will be the fast beating the slow."—Rupert Murdock[15]

In certain areas of work, it's ok to lead from it's **good enough**. It will never be perfect. Think about things like web pages that aren't perfect, and may never be, or products that might be good, but not 100% perfect. If we wait to put them out in the world, it may be obsolete, with our client needs already having shifted.

In my line of work and working with groups, a lot of my own business has come through "getting out there," speaking with people, building relationships with people whether it's been paid, or it's been pro bono. In today's business context, it's possible to "get out there" virtually and this can include social media and websites.

There are many ways to get out there with our message. Questions to consider:

1. *What does GETTING OUT THERE mean for you?*

      _____

      _____

      _____

2. *What are the messages you want to communicate?*

      _____

      _____

      _____

3. *What online visibility do you want to create?*

      _____

      _____

4. *What does consistent mean for you? Posting weekly? Daily? Three times a week? Often?*

      _____

      _____

5. *What is your plan? Consider using the Content Checklist and referring to the Content Calendar.*

      _____

      _____

6. *What metrics do you want to track?*

      _____

      _____

15 http://www.azquotes.com/quote/209311

The Sparker—Jenn's Story

An important experiment I've undertaken around visibility started back on January 1, 2014 with what was originally going to be a one-year or 365-day blogging project around the area of team leadership. Some of you have met me through my earliest blogs around group and team coaching, or maybe even work-life issues. I've been a blogger since 2005.

At the start of 2014, I really wanted to be offering more to the leadership sphere. I also wanted to raise the profile of our Potentials Realized website which was only getting 80 page views a day back in December 2013! Now in the spring of 2018, the same site received more than 10,250 page views this week.

So, on January 1, 2014, I launched the Teams365 blog at PotentialsRealized.com. It's geared for team leaders and their teams. We're well beyond 1,600 posts in the fifth year of the blog and that work has become an important vehicle for my work with teams, leaders, and all things virtual. It's become an important way for me to continue shaping my own voice, and building content for my clients' needs, growing visibility for my own brand.

As you'll see at the Teams365 blog the posts are not super long. It really is to facilitate and spark a conversation for leaders and their teams. One thing it's enabled for me is a whole slew of new networks. Looking at spring business that's coming in the door from large companies that I've never met before, many of them indicated that they found me online. So, I think that actually speaks volumes to having visibility as a web presence.

So, whether it's virtual, whether it's live, whether we're doing networking or we're doing educational marketing, I think it's important for us to think about a few questions.

Question #1: **What does getting out there mean for you and what's it going to take?**

_____

_____

Question #2: **What's important for you to take action on?** *As you think about today and what's important in your world of work, what are the one or two things you want to take action on?*

_____

_____

It's easy to create "an over-to-do" list. I love making to-do lists, but there's only so much we can put attention around. What would it be like to focus on a handful of ideas where you can see movement rather than working through a big laundry list?

In the planner section you'll see this concept where you are first invited to capture all your daily or quarterly tasks on a master list (what's often called a Task List or a Rapid Log in the world of Bullet Journals). Then you are invited to break these down into monthly goals, weekly goals, highlighting the top 5 or 3 across the board or more specifically.

Here are some questions to consider, and feel free to flip to the planner section to write them out there

> Section 5 Tools: You will want to use the Monthly To-Do – Task List on a monthly basis to brainstorm and capture monthly task ideas, or the To-Do Section of the Quarterly Planner to capture quarterly tasks.

Question #3: **Keeping this in mind, WHO do you want to become more visible to?** *What relationships, what areas do you want to get to this year?*

_____

_____

Question #4: **What could visibility look like?** *Where do you want to get out more? Keeping your major goals in mind, where do we want to position ourselves?*

_____

_____

_____

Question #5: **In building a business what strengths can you bring to this?**

_____

_____

Question #6: **Ultimately what is important for you to take action on?**

_____

_____

What is important if you look at the next quarter or by the end of the year?

_____

_____

Now, considering your vision, and as you think about getting there, what is your master list?

_____

_____

_____

If we're trying to fit ourselves in molds that just don't work, that are uncomfortable for us or that are really outside of our comfort zone, it's probably not going to be sustainable. —Jennifer Britton

Sustainability is a theme I hope you picked up in the tips of the Solopreneur Primer. We do want to make sure that we're leveraging our strengths and are able to sustain the business and pace for the long term. There have been a lot of coaching questions here, so please take a few minutes to stop, pause, and reflect on the questions included. Enjoy!

Lead and Serve

Solopreneur tip seven is **lead and serve**. As professionals, we don't always stop to think about what's happening and what's going on, but these are critical for success. Our businesses are often a reflection of who we are, and we are regularly called to lead and serve.

Think about your business. How is it a reflection of who you are?

_____

_____

How do you want to lead? Who do you want to serve? How can your business enable this?

_____

_____

_____

_____

The Sparker—Jenn's Story

My business is a huge part of who I am, who I have been all my life. Many of you have heard me talk about my roots as an experiential educator up in Algonquin Park. I was very privileged to be able to spend my summers as a university student, working in the Park. I was responsible for leading a staff team of about a dozen swim instructors each summer. The world was ahead of me, but really, I have always been very privileged to work with amazing, amazing teams.

I think of the next phase of leadership as my global phase. What I thought would be a three-month, overseas placement became the anchor for almost thirteen years of work globally. In my work with Canadian and British organizations and the United Nations, leading and serving was critical. From working at the grassroots community level to working with regional governments, my work as a program manager and director involved empowering others so they could lead and serve in their organizations, communities, and nations. My work was about relationships and I continue to love the work that I do.

Today, I get to connect people in all the work that I do. Whether it's hosting a webinar, group coaching session or an in-person meeting, much of my work is connecting others for conversation around issues they are interested in.

For me, leadership has always been key. Whether I've been a formal leader, whether I've been serving, you know, different populations, different communities—I was very privileged to work on everything from educational projects to health care to sea turtle research. I've built schools and ecotourism trails. Throughout my work I've had a lot of adventures and success, but it was not just about me. It was really the web of relationships that I was able to build and people that I was able to work through.

Even now I measure my work in terms of impact and connection with others. Someone the other day asked me, **what's the benefit of writing a book**? I think the scope, the magnitude, the outreach my books have been so much more than I could've ever imagined. My first book, *Effective Group Coaching* has now been translated into Polish, and my books are being used by business schools, and coaching programs all over the world.

I've spent a lot of time, as I said in the last lesson, building relationships, getting out there, being in dialogue and being in communication with people and so it's really, it's fed me, but it's also served the business as well.

So, I would like you to think about your leadership:

What legacy do you want to leave?

_____

_____

What and who do you want to serve?

_____

_____

What impact do you want to make?

_____

_____

Think about these three questions and think about, as a business owner, what are the spheres in which you want to lead? The world is a very big place, our clients are everywhere, but who are the people that you really want to serve?

Client Preferences

Tip number eight is listen to what your clients want and need.

Our clients are instructive. They can really lead us to great products and programs if we listen to them. And that's what we do as coaches. We listen for what our clients want and need. We're asking them questions. What's going to help you? What support do you need? Your clients will probably direct you to some great ideas for products and services over time.

Be listening for what your clients really need. You might listen for:

- Do they want long programs? Do they want short programs?
- What pricing is going to work for them?
- What makes sense in terms of their support needs? Is it coaching? Is it training? Is it something else?

What do your clients really, really need? Listen deeply to that, listen to how those needs change, check it out. Involving them continues to build on many of these tips that we've looked at already.

I'd like to invite you to use your client base as a barometer. Going forward, be intentional in listening to what they need. And from that data, in collaboration with them, think through what those offerings are that you want to bring out to the world. I hope that you will avoid the "analysis paralysis" place. We want to be asking questions, but there is a point at which there may be too much information. So use your intuition, go with your gut, listen to your trusted advisors, listen to your past clients in terms of what they like and love about your work, and really think about how you can leverage your strengths, how you can get out there and offer what you want.

The Sparker—Jenn's Story

I look at almost every program that I've offered to the public in the last 14 years, whether it was a 90-day Biz Success program or the 90 day Your Balanced Life™ program and how it's been shaped by client needs.

One of the most recent ones that was shaped by client requests is the Learning Lab and Design Studio—a full year of ongoing group coaching program for coaches, trainers, facilitators to work with me in both a group context and an individual context. For years I've had coaches come out of the Group Coaching Essentials, and then move on to the Advanced Group and Team Coaching Practicum. After that, several then said I want to work with you longer term. That's where the Learning Lab and Design Studio came about.

There is usually never an optimum time to start a new program. In early 2015 I said, 'I've got to start this. If I don't start it now, when am I going to start it?'

It's been really fun. Week to week to week I have built the program over three years. Yes, it's taken some time, but as usual I've been able to iterate and design on the fly. That is one of my strengths. I rarely have a halt in business, so I look to quieter months like December and January to get the infrastructure up and running. That allows me to build programming each and every week, in a very client-centric, iterative way.

This year in 2018, I've headed down the path again, building as I go with my newest "Lab" program—the Coaching Biz Growth Lab™. This group is a dedicated space for coaches wanting to start, or grow, their businesses. I hope that you will consider joining us!

Activity:

Take stock of what your clients want and need. What have they been asking for lately?

Make a list of 5-10 possible new services, products, or offerings you could create:

1. _____

2. _____

3. _____

4. _____

5. _____

6. _____

7. _____

8. _____

9. _____

10. _____

Step back and weigh them based on what's important to your business. Is it to scale the number of people you work with, or is it to generate more revenue? What is important?

Have Fun and Do What You Like

What's the lifestyle you want to create?

One of the most important things I have learned since I opened the doors is that it is critical to have fun and do what we love. The work of a small business owner today is not easy. There are competing demands. There are times when we're going to have to work through weekends, start early and log off late. Hopefully, we are doing what we love so it doesn't feel like a chore. It's not uncommon to enroll my family in the lead up to big events and it allows us to spend quality time together.

It's important that we get clear on what's fun and do what we love to do because entrepreneurship is not for everyone. Small business ownership is not for everyone. Some of my friends look at me and think, how do you do it? Do you really love what you do? But they know that I do. While I work long hours at times of the year, at other times in my work I have amazing flexibility so that I can work out of beautiful Muskoka, Canada for two months of the year. They also know that there are times when I push it. One of the reasons why I have continued to do a lot of virtual work is that it does allow me to connect with people like you all over the world and I don't have to travel.

When I first recorded this tip I had just returned from travel to the Canadian Prairies to do an in-person program. I loved it and would love to do more, but I also look at the time it took to travel. It was three days and while I really enjoyed it I know that at my current stage of life I don't have the energy anymore to be able to do that each and every week. Perhaps you do and maybe that's what fun is for you.

At this juncture, coaching questions you might consider are:

Where are we in our stage of life?

What are our current commitments and what's going to be fun?

What's going to create excitement, and not dread?

Think about what FUN means and what you love to do.

_____

_____

How can you put out the intention for more FUN in your work?

_____

_____

What's the lifestyle you want to create?

_____

_____

Creating Undeniable Value

Tip #10 is all about creating or providing undeniable value.

Before you continue, I want you to think about the term—**undeniable value**.

What does that mean?

What does that mean **for you**?

What does it mean for **your clients**?

What **do they** find valuable?

Key to the work that we undertake is adding value. We can add value as a coach in many different ways—through the pause that we create, through great customer service, through holding attention on what's important, and by being a partner with our clients.

A couple more questions for you to consider:

What is the value you bring through your work?

_____

_____

What are the three adjectives that describe your value?

_____

_____

You may want to go out and ask clients, people that you've worked with, friends, colleagues, what do they see as your value and sift through those, really take stock of what you hear and then connect with what you think is your value.

Look at your work and if you do any evaluations or testimonials, it can be very interesting to lay out the data you have received, and the feedback you've received.

What do people consistently say?

_____

_____

What are they saying now that is different from what they've said before?

_____

_____

What do you want to be known for?

_____

_____

Many of these tips in this section of the solopreneur primer is about your niche. Your brand at the end of the day is YOU! As solopreneurs our business is who we are. Our work is a reflection of us.

So, what is the value that you want to create?

What is important for you in terms of your legacy and your impact?

What Do Your <u>Client's</u> Value?

Part two of tip 10 is what do your clients really value. Do you listen and check your assumptions about what you are hearing. I think it's very easy for us to put a lens on and think "this is valuable, or this is not valuable." Be listening. What you value may not be what your clients value.

Unfortunately, there continues to be a lot of noise in the marketplace for solopreneurs. "You have to do this. You have to do that. You need to be on social media."

This noise can be too much for some coaches who move to overwhelm. Part of the intent of this book is to allow you to take a step-by-step approach to work through these questions, one at a time.

I want you to think about what's important for you. One of the key approaches can be to build things over time. Businesses are not built overnight. Someone recently said, "You've created so much." I responded, "It's built up over time." It's amazing to see how they all sort of dovetail together. One of the things I've intentionally done each year is to develop a new product or book or other creative initiatives. It is often that my summer months are the pause point to be able to sit down, focus, and build over time. Over time we can really build the foundations of our business. Take a look at some of the last five year's product offerings which have been influenced by client needs.

> Annual Product Launches:
>
> 2018 CBB Planner Caoaching Biz Growth Lab
>
> 2017: *Effective Virtual Conversations* (Book)
>
> 2016: Learning Lab and Design Studio
>
> 2015: 40 Ways to Work with Visual Cards
>
> 2014: Conversation Sparker
>
> 2013: *From One to Many: Best Practices for Team and Group Coaching*

In terms of marketing and making sure that we are tapping into what our clients value, it is important to be consistent. Be consistent with your messaging, be consistent in your ads, with your brand.

What does consistency mean for you?

_____

_____

Think about the consistency. Consistency doesn't mean that you can't do different things and that you have to do the same thing all the time. It is important that people see how things tie together. Consider what you've created when products can be developed into other projects or purposes. Part of this may be to consider how you can reduce, reuse, and recycle.

Here's what I wrote in a blog post at the Group Coaching Ins and Outs called the *3 Rs to Group Program Development*[16]:

1. **Reduce**—Follow the "Less is More" principle. Rather than trying to fit everything, including the kitchen sink, into your next workshop set at least 20% of the content aside. This content can be used as the foundation for a new program or as follow-up to your program. Participants will thank you as they avoid overwhelm, information overload, and have a chance to really engage with, and integrate the material you provide.
   What program content can you reduce or practice the 80/20 rule on?

2. **Reuse**—*What programs are you currently offering? How could you leverage and repackage these program offerings so that they could be delivered to a wider audience?*

   For example, over the years I have developed a number of different streams of group programs—the Your Balanced Life™ program, and the 90 Day Biz Success™ program for business owners. I offer these programs in a number of different formats including a 90-day group coaching program by phone, a weekend retreat, a virtual retreat, short-term speaking engagements and also corporate workshops. The skeleton and main content for each of these programs is the same, it's just put together in different delivery options with changes to meet the needs of different groups.

---

16 http://groupcoaching.blogspot.ca/2008/01/3-rs-to-group-program-development.html (accessed 5.1.18)

What programs can you reuse to meet the needs of different audiences? How could you deliver some of your current programs differently?

3. **Recycle**—I often talk about using the modular approach to program development where discrete, mini-sessions are developed as separate entities, which can then be put together with other modules to create entirely new programs, depending on the needs of the audience.

Think about modular program development like building blocks of different pieces of LEGO˙. You may have a one-hour module on Developing Your Vision, a one-hour module on leadership, a one-hour module on providing feedback, and one on values. Depending on the needs of the client, or the group you are developing your program for, you can select different LEGO˙ pieces or building blocks to create an entirely different structure. With a few small tweaks to further customize, you've got a new program there!

What modules do you already have on hand? What can you construct from what you have right now?

Activity:

Think about your own work and the content you have created. Complete the following chart:

Intellectual property I have (Presentations, Worksheets, Blogs, Podcasts)	What do people like about it or what do they find useful?	How else could I repackage it?	How else could I repurpose it?

After you have generated your list, what are your next steps? Anything to add to your One Page Plan?

Continuous Learning—Keep Fresh

In today's world of VUCA—Volatility, Uncertainty, Complexity, and Ambiguity, it's really important to continuously learn. Our client's worlds are always changing, as is our own world by extension.

So, lesson number 11 is about keeping fresh. My first question to you is *how fresh are your skills?* What is challenging and stretching you in your work right now?

As solopreneurs, we may be challenged in different ways by:

- adding on new programs
- increasing volume of work
- collaborating with larger entities
- keeping fresh through on-going or continuous learning

One of the questions I'd like you to sort of hold as an inquiry is, "Looking ahead, what skills and experiences do you want to acquire or hone?"

It can be useful to revisit the skills assessment you did in Section 1. Check back to it and add these to the space below.

Activity:
List the skills you need to run and grow the business. Add on any additional skill sets you think are necessary. Get granular with specific skills in each area, for example, under marketing include graphic design and creating blog post images.

Coaching Skills	Administrative Skills	Program Design	Marketing	Financial
Other	Other			

After you have generated your own list, place a check beside the ones you are good at. Put a circle around the skills that are not your strengths. Notice what areas you want to grow your skills in. Consider adding these to your One Page Plan.

Now, keeping fresh is great, but I think it's also important to ask ourselves **how much is enough**? If we don't use it, do we lose it? Coaching is a skill set that if we're not in front of clients all the time, we do lose those skills. Atrophy happens.

Part of keeping it fresh is listening to what clients want and what they need, and designing from there. It is also making sure that we avoid analysis paralysis by getting into action. I continue to meet a lot of coaches who sort of suffer from over-study syndrome. They want to keep it fresh so they're constantly adding to their toolbox, but they're not necessarily **using** the different tools and skills that they have at their fingertips.

Themes in this section were:

- What does it mean to keep it fresh?
- What do your clients want?
- What can you put into action or practice?

Keeping this in mind, what learning and growth experiences do you want to undertake this quarter and this year? Schedule them into your planner.

_____

_____

It's All Yours!

This final tip for the section is "It is all yours!" The business is yours as solopreneur. As someone who is running their own business, really at the end of the day, this business is yours. You are the foundation of success, failure, and learning.

As you have moved through the workbook I hope you have had the chance to get clearer on what your business is all about. You can also refine your business, as your needs change, or as your family needs change, and how you want to contribute in the world.

We started off this journey back in lesson number one by asking you, **"What do you really want to create?"**

And at that time, I invited you to do some work around your vision.

Here we have nine of the photo cards from the Conversation Sparker™ Deck. Select one of the photos that represents what you see as your vision for your business. This business is your own. What is it that you want to create in your work?

The photo I selected is:

_____

What it represents for me:

_____

_____

What is important for me to note?

_____

_____

What action can I take from this place?

_____

_____

As I was going about selecting photos for the Conversation Sparker™ deck I loved thinking about which photos would call people to new awareness and action.

Looking at these photos, the window shot at the bottom right invites us to think about the many different facets that make up our work. I've had people comment on the sunrise or sunset photo as being the landscape for possibility. Perhaps you want to be like the tall tree covered in ice, reaching for the sky, or maybe you want to just sit a spell and sit and enjoy the flowers. Perhaps you're looking for the pot of the rainbow at the end of the rainbow as in the top right corner, or maybe you just want to go and "chillax" by the ocean. The business is yours. What perspective do you want to step in?

I hope that this section has gotten you thinking more clearly about what you want to create in your business. I'd invite you to share that with those around you so that they can support you in your ongoing journey.

Make a claim, take a stance around what it is that you want to create, and most importantly, share with your loved ones. We spend an awful lot of time growing our businesses.

End-of-Section Checkpoint

What are the key items you want to remember from this section?

_____

_____

What do you want to add to your plans?

_____

_____

What has become really clear for you so far?

_____

_____

_____

Section 3

Marketing Essentials

In addition to the other section of this book, this section includes some of the foundational essentials to promotion and marketing, as well as developing a business plan.

Developing a Business Plan

Do you have a business plan? Planning is key. As a business owner, if we have no plan, if we don't know where we are, it's really hard to maintain a thriving, not just a sustaining, business.

Business plans are not only useful tools for leveraging much needed capital, but they can be invaluable tools for business owners. A business plan should be a living, breathing document that is regularly updated and referred to.

This is the heart of any coaching business, and it's likely that for some, this becomes the heart of your work.

Much of what we are working through can become enshrined in a more formal business plan. While not every business is going to take time to develop this, it can be a very useful exercise.

What should a business plan include?

Some of the core elements—working front to back include:

A **table of contents** and an **executive summary**. The executive summary is generally written at the end, after all other elements are complete.

It should also include a business and management overview. Who is running the company? How has it been established?

What's your marketing plan? This is something that I hope you'll start adding onto with marketing.

The marketing section includes your four Ps—your **pricing, your product** and service offering, your **promotion,** and where you're **putting** it.

How are you **distributing** things? Is it digital? Is it in stores, on your website, or on other digital sites like Amazon?

Exploring the Context

If you're going for any capital, most banks will want you to do a bit of an **industry analysis**. This could include market review or research, asking yourself:

- How big is the industry?
- Who are the major players?
- What are key themes and trends?
- What opportunities and threats exist?

In the next section, we'll be exploring some of this through the SWOT tool, which you are invited to engage in at the level of your business and the level of your industry.

As business owners it is really important to get a lay of the land. Here's where strategic planning tools will help you do some of that analysis. Strategic planning helps you identify your competitors, explore what's happening in the industry, identify key themes and similar existing products?

Other traditional business plan sections include:

Personnel requirements—Who is your team? Employees, subcontractors, others who help with the day-to-day operations and management of your business. We'll be looking at some of this initially through the Top 20 Worksheet.

Legal requirements will vary from location to location. What local experts can provide you the legal advice you need and require in order to run a business?

Financial requirements will also vary from business to business. What experts can help you in this area?

In addition to the overarching business plan, you will want to create a living, breathing plan. Planning can happen on multiple levels—annual, quarterly, monthly, and daily. You will note the different planner pages in Section 5. You are encouraged to use these on a consistent basis.

A plan is only as good as its execution. Are you building in time regularly for reflection and planning? Perhaps, on a quarterly basis, look at all of the key themes, priorities for that format.

Five Essential Coaching Business Systems

Business systems help a business flow and also help with automation and scaling or growth of a coaching business.

How do we define a system? A system is something we can replicate. Systems are useful for things we repeatedly do. They enable us to have multiple programs and services being offered at any one time. They also allow us to delegate and hand off items to others. From a high level, there are multiple areas we might develop systems around including:

1. Sales and marketing
2. Product and program services
3. Registration and client onboarding supports
4. Financial systems
5. Communication

These are several areas I think you might find important to look at, from a high level:

Area #1—Sales and Marketing

I put sales and marketing up at the top because if people don't know about us, if people can't find us, if people can't pay us, we really go out of business very, very quickly. What is it that you are offering?

Sales

Sales is different than marketing. Marketing involves promotion and letting the world know about what you have to offer. Sales is about closing the transaction. As solopreneurs, we want to make sure that we are tracking our sales, as well as our marketing efforts.

On the sales level you might have systems to track

- sales made (amount, to whom, when),
- inventory,
- when items need a refill

You may also create order forms, invoicing, and payment trackers.

What systems do you want to create in the areas of sales?

_____

_____

_____

Marketing

Marketing systems can help to automate some of the marketing work you are doing. For example, getting the word out or considering how your content can be syndicated.

On the marketing level, coaches may have systems to:

> Check out the 101 Marketing Ideas download at the CoachingBusinessBuilder.com

- Create content (i.e. blog posts, newsletters, brochures)
- Distribute content—Check out the content related planning tools in Section 5. Common systems include content schedulers (annual, monthly, weekly), tracking (use the Monthly Daily Tracker to capture when you are posting and/or post reads).
- Schedule and track announcements about your services
- Schedule and track other marketing initiatives such as speaking or webinars (when, how many attended, feedback received, sales made)

What marketing systems do you have in place? What ones do you want to create?

_____

_____

_____

Area #2—Product and Program Services

As coaches, we may be building several different revenue streams. From passive revenue e-books to live workshops and retreats, becoming well versed on program and product services is key. While this is not a replacement for a more extensive learning process, it is important to note that program development consists of several different stages.

Let's consider the example of Lisa, a new coach who is wanting to bring to life a new group-coaching program. As she goes to consider what she is about to offer, she goes through several stages of the group-coaching program development process including design, delivery, evaluation, and sustainability.

Program Development:

"The emerging discipline of program management gives professionals the knowledge and skills necessary to think big picture and understand the benefits of leveraging the interdependencies between projects." –Zinn, HR Reporter, November 2008

Coaches may find themselves involved in program development on multiple levels. From the design and marketing of their own group coaching work, to designing presentations for lunch and learns, to designing team coaching programs, program development is an important, and often overlooked, area of business development.

Program development usually consists of several steps and will involve exploring questions such as:

Pre-program: Pre-program communication with your audience is critical for success. Questions you will want to consider: Who is the program for? What are their needs? What is the purpose of the program? What outcomes are people looking for? Throughout my work as a group coach, I like to meet with group members for a short 15-minute pre-call to learn more about them, what's brought them to the program and what their coaching goals are.

What pre-program activities do you want to include in your work?

_____

_____

Design: The design of a program includes the different program elements (calls, videos, field work, worksheets). This can vary significantly according to the types of programs you are creating, and your clients.

What program elements will support the goals of the clients/coachees? What brand does the program have?

_____

_____

Delivery: Program delivery gets you thinking about how the program will be accessed.

Will the program be delivered live (virtual or in-person) or will it be an on-demand program (video-based program, email program, or e-learning program) which people can take at their own pace?

_____

_____

Evaluation: *What will you do to evaluate the program and adjust it as you go?*

_____

_____

Regular checkpoints to take stock of things is critical. In most programs, and individual coaching work, I like to schedule at minimum a mid-point review or some checkpoint generally every quarter.

During these mid-point evaluations, you may want to explore these questions:

Questions to Consider:

- What is the progress toward the key program objectives and indicators?
- What major opportunities exist? How can these be leveraged?
- What problems exist? What is needed to address them?
- How are the actual costs comparing to the planned costs?
- What would you do differently about the program if you could do anything?
- What limitations are holding you back from what you would ideally do?
- What are you learning from the program implementation so far?
- What lessons learned should be taken forward?

Sustainability: *What will support the ongoing change, learning and action of the program clients? What follow-up is required? Will you schedule in follow-up calls, or booster shots throughout the year?*

_____

_____

A related topic to program development is product development. This will be of interest to coaches who are looking for additional revenue streams.

Area #3—Client Onboarding and Registration Systems:

Welcoming our clients starts at their first contact, which may be through a visit to our website, hearing us speak, or through referral. You will want to think about how your clients find you and get enrolled in the process.

Often coaches set up a "sample" session or "discovery" session to meet with the client to meet the client, learn more about their coaching to see if there is a fit between what they offer and what the clients needs.

Two common areas systems can be developed in are:

> If you're thinking of offering workshops, retreats, or group coaching, I go into much greater depth on this topic around registration and invoicing and communication In the Tips for Your Team and Group Programs resource.

- Registration
- Outreach and promotion

Registration Systems

There are myriad options for registering people, ranging from your website, PayPal, or Eventbrite.

How will people be able to find out AND register for your program?

What will you do to track registrations? Capture attendee names and contacts?

_____

_____

Outreach and Promotion

How are people going to find you?

What are the major promotional strategies you want to employ? From social media, to speaking, to article writing, I cover more on 10 different strategies later in this Section.

_____

_____

Once people have registered, we then want to welcome them to our services.

For individual clients, our onboarding support may include some or all of these:

- A sample session—what are the things you want to do during this phase
- A welcome letter and package. While these can vary they may include: Your Terms and Conditions or Agreements—what is being offered, what coaching is and is not, how you will bill, what happens if sessions are missed. The role of the client and role of the coach.
- A journal or other welcome materials
- Agreements
- What people can expect—Be clear on what you are offering. This might include some of the elements included in Frequently Asked Questions OR it may include more detail about pre-work
- Frequently Asked Questions
- Confirmation of the first session

Frequently Asked Questions:

Frequently Asked Question (FAQ) sheets can be very useful in providing more details about your program. FAQs can be posted on your website as a download link or sent out to participants. Frequently asked questions may include:

How can I participate? *Is this an in-person or online program?*

Where is the program held? *Provide participants with details around course location (online or in person)*

What do I need to participate? *What materials and technology do people need to participate? Do they need access to the internet? Is there any software required?*

What time will be required for people to participate? *What are the expectations from you in terms of amount of time required for assignments, readings, preparation before the next session, etc.?*

How do I connect/access the calls and/or information? *Include any details and testing required prior to the start of the program. Indicate what people need to have done, and WHEN, before the start of the program.*

As a participant, what supports will I have? *Include information on materials provided, access to you and other participants*

What components are included in their registration? *Provide details in your FAQ—the program itself— length, start and end times; any follow-up coaching, follow-up calls.*

Activity:

- Draft your FAQ. What else do you want to include in your FAQ?
- How do you want to make this available to your participants (Email, web, other)?

Area #4—Financial Systems

As a business owner you'll become a lot more familiar with financial issues than you likely have throughout your career.

Maybe it's things that you want to have in place this week, this month, or this quarter. In opening your doors, people will have to be able to pay you, so make sure you get money and banking issues in place early on. This may also involve business registration and insurance needs. Reaching out to your local small business centers (www.sba.gov in the US), as well as your local ICF chapter, can provide some important tips and insights as to what is required in your local area. This can vary drastically from location to location.

Make sure you know what you need to do from a money standpoint. This may require reaching out to an accountant, a lawyer, and also looking into taxation systems in your local area, as well as where your clients reside.

What is the research and action you want to undertake around this?

Some of the issues you will want to consider early on are:

- What is your legal business structure?
- What do you need to do to register your business? (local/ federal)
- Banking systems—establishing a business bank account
- Taxation issues

How are customers going to be able to pay you? Are you going to have PayPal, Stripe, or Square or some other online payment system?

A business is only as viable as its financial base. What are the different streams you have which will ensure cash flow during the natural ebbs and flows of business?

If you have been in business for a while, consider when is cash flow strong, and when is it not.

> For more on this topic refer to Marketing Tips for your Group and Team Programs.
>
> This five-hour on-demand program goes into more detail around many of these different promotional strategies, blogging, speaking, article writing, so whether we are looking at developing group and team programs or looking at developing more of a following.

Area #5—Communication Systems

Communication is the name of the game with our work. Some months I have been known to spend thousands of minutes on the phone and web. How are you communicating with people? Systems in this area means getting your house in order around "all things communication." From phone to web, to looking at bridge lines, having a Webinar host or zoom room, and, if you are using a phone considering long distance packages.

Activity:

Make a list of what you need. What are the communication systems you think you will find useful?

_____

_____

Promotional Vehicles—Beyond Social Media

One of the most important, and immediate things, coaches think about when starting a business is promotional vehicles. Developing a variety of promotional vehicles for your business is an important part of building your brand and expanding your work. It is important that we get the word out about what we have to offer. Promotion is just one part of marketing and does not necessarily lead to a sale.

This section is going to explore some of the more common promotional vehicles coaches employ.

As a starting point I'd like you to think of your clients:

- Who are they?
- What do they prefer?
- Where are they going to look for information about services and support for themselves?

The approaches and strategies people will use will be different if you're working with a baby boomer versus a millennial. It will look different whether you're promoting to an HR director versus a small-business owner. As we go through this section, I'd like you to keep in mind **the strategies and different vehicles that will be useful to the clients that you work with.**

> Reminder to revisit the Client Profile in Section 2

Also think about yourself. Put yourself in the equation here. As business owners, we want to make sure that we're using strategies that will work well for who we are. If we're doing things that don't work well or don't really draw on our strengths, are we going to continue doing them? Absolutely not. We will drop them by the wayside.

Critical for success in marketing is **consistency**. In marketing it is essential to consistently undertake action, whether you're new to your business or whether your business is well established. Promotion is also something that we want to continue doing. The third area which is key is developing relationships. We never want to think that we are finished building relationships. Coaching is all about people and relationships.

> **The Seven to Eleven Times Rule** asserts that it takes someone seven to eleven times of hearing, or seeing, something before it registers and they start to ask if they need an item. What are the seven to eleven touchpoints you want to create for your product or service?

Having a variety of outreach and promotional strategies is also important. Just as in the 3 R Rule—Reduce, Reuse, and Recycle—a message on one channel (for example, an article) can quickly be repurposed on another. Keep this in mind as you explore the next few pages. Vehicles and messaging can, and should be related, or at least connected.

There are several promotional strategies that coaches will employ in getting the word out about their services:

Strategy #1—Speaking

While speaking may not be for everyone, it is a great way to get out in front of people—virtually or in person. It is a way to connect with large and small audiences. As a speaker you may be showing up to speak at events that others organize, or some you may be organizing the event yourself (webinars, lunch and learns at a community center).

You'll want to think about those speaking topics that would be of interest to people with whom you are looking to develop networks.

We always want to have a message that's resonant to the people that we are looking to connect with and we want to make sure that it's polished and professional.

Activity—Make a list of speaking topics you could give. Identify places, conferences, associations, or areas where you could speak.

Things to consider around speaking:

- Topics
- Venues
- Type of presentation
- Virtual or in person
- Large group, small group
- How interactive do you want to make it?
- How does it connect to the services you are offering?
- What speaking supports do you want to create? For example, a Speaking One Page, or a downloadable brochure event planners can access.

Tips for Powerful Presentations

As business owners we are involved in several different presentations throughout the day. From one-on-one conversations about what we have to offer, to group or team sessions, honing our skills in presentations can be important.

Things to keep in mind when designing and leading presentations:

Open, body, close. Presentations usually have these three parts – the opening, which usually sets the stage for the conversation. The body or bulk of what you want to share (approximately 80%) and the close which includes your call to action and summary of what you've covered (approximately 10%).

Due to the **latency** and **recency effect** of the brain we tend to remember the start and end of a presentation. What are you doing to connect people early on with what's important to them about this topic? What are you doing to review or reinforce the points you have covered?

Purpose—What is the purpose of the presentation? Is it to share information or educate? Is it to influence behavior? Is it to foster dialogue?

Three bullet points—We remember a fixed amount of information. Becoming crisp with our conversation and highlighting key messages in bullet points can keep things flowing. What are your three bullet points?

Activity:

Make a list of 10 topics you could speak about.

_____

_____

_____

_____

_____

_____

_____

_____

_____

_____

Strategy #2—Blogging

Blogging is a valuable strategy for increasing visibility. When a blog is attached to your site it becomes an essential calling card. Blogging is beneficial as it can help to:

- Grow your following or audience
- Find your voice and create your message
- Act as a resource for clients to refer to

Going hand in hand with speaking is blogging. Some of us may prefer to connect by audio. That is the speaking. Whereas others of us like to write, and I've been a blogger for the last 10 years.

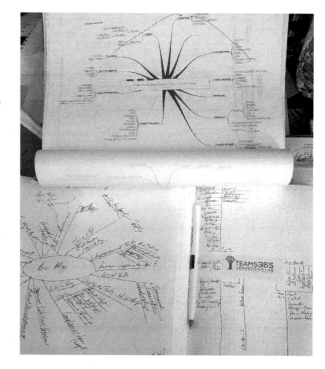

Blogging is a great way to connect and educate the people that you're working with as coaches. As coaches, our role is not necessarily there to train or educate people. Blogging is a go-to resource site for people to follow-up on. You might include themes or topics that you'd been looking at.

Historically, blogging is great in terms of search engine optimization given that content is refreshed regularly. This may include blogging on related topics, using key words. Blogging can be an important vehicle to develop thought leadership and refine your message.

Having a place to point people back to is critical in social media, and blogging is an important hub of this.

As a seasoned blogger I know how important it is to have a plan. MindMaps have been my go-to starting point to capture ideas. It has become the resource touchpoint in the event of writer's block. Take a look at the photo above of three MindMaps for three of my writing and design projects.

Activity:

1. Make a list or MindMap all of the blog topics that come to mind.

2. Step back—What else could you add, knowing your client?

_____

_____

_____

_____

_____

_____

_____

_____

_____

_____

_____

_____

_____

_____

_____

_____

_____

_____

Five Questions to Consider from a Serial Blogger

As someone who has hosted blogs since 2005, and uses blogging as a way to educate, share ideas, and create content, I thought it would be fitting to share five questions to consider as you start blogging:

#1. **What's the purpose of the blog?** Why are you embarking on this adventure? Is it to have a structure to develop content, refine your writing, have a place for your clients to go for resources, curate information, develop thought leadership or other?

The purpose of my blog is to: _____

#2. Who is it for? Your audience will further shape the type of posts and length of posts.

_____

_____

My audience wants:

_____

_____

#3. What do you want to write about? Have a list of ideas you can write about. Writer's block does happen!

Different ideas for blog posts are:

- An A to Z around a topic, for example, the A to Z of Virtual Team Activities (one that I created and sell)
- 10 resources to consider around x topic
- A day in the life
- Behind the scenes
- Common questions
- Pitfalls and how to mitigate
- Books to read
- Websites to visit
- What's important on this topic

   10 items I could write about are:

   _____   _____

   _____   _____

   _____   _____

   _____   _____

   _____   _____

#4. Be consistent and have a plan—What's your schedule? What are your topics? Take the 10 minutes to develop a MindMap (as previously suggested) given that a part of consistency is having context

   _I want to blog ____ a _____ (week/month/day/year)_

_____

Topics I definitely want to blog about are:

_____

_____

_____

#5. **When will you write?** In sustaining a daily blog for almost five years I spend several blocks a month writing specifically for the blog. During the last week of the month I outline the blog posts I am going to write, and I tend to write in two morning blocks each week, scheduling the content for later distribution.

When do you want to write? What do you need to do to make this happen?

_____

_____

_____

Strategy #3—Podcasting

Returning to the auditory or verbal channel, another related promotional vehicle is podcasting. Podcasting has recently come back with a vengeance given the advent of personal speakers.

According to Edison Research, **67 million Americans listen to podcasts monthly, an increase of** 14 percent in one year[17].

You don't necessarily have to host your own podcast. You could be a speaker who is a guest at other's podcasts and events. I would encourage you to just google the term podcasting. There's a lot of great resources out there. It's another way to connect with people in your prospective audience.

With the tsunami of smart speaker devices like Alexa and Google Home, more people may be turning to audio content from these devices in the future.

In terms of integrating podcasting as a strategy, you can host your own or be a guest and work through others. Where does your interest reside?

Activity:

Do some research. What podcasts exist around your topic?

_____

_____

_____

17 http://www.edisonresearch.com/infinite-dial-2017/

Who hosts podcasts on the topics you work around? What are key podcasts you could show up on and be a guest on?

_____

_____

_____

Strategy #4—Networking

Networking is another promotional vehicle. Think about who your network is. Are you networking with a global audience where networking is going to look different than going to your local chamber of commerce? Think about how you can connect with people in that perspective. Who is the audience? What is important to them. Knowing your audience and connecting with them is central to developing rich relationships through networking. It's not always about numbers. It really is more about connection points and the depth of those potential relationships.

Tips for Networking and Relationship Building

- Consider what events you want to attend
- Know why you want to attend an event
- What is your intention?
- Who can support you in your work and outreach?
- Who are the connectors who can connect you with others?

Activity:

Make a list of the top 20 people you have in your network. This might include: A Virtual Assistant, Bloggers, Coaches, Marketing Experts, Legal or Financial Advisors, etc.

_____   _____

_____   _____

_____   _____

_____   _____

_____   _____

_____   _____

_____   _____

_____   _____

_____   _____

_____   _____

As you refer to your list, who are influencers? Who is missing? Who do you need to be "more in front of"? What could this look like?

_____

_____

Strategy #5—Article Writing

A fifth area to look at is article writing. It's another way to get your message out into the world. Whether you are posting your articles on LinkedIn or you're a guest writer for a a larger subscription base, it's a great way to get word out about what you have to offer.

Article writing is also a great way to educate others. When being interviewed by media, it is common to be asked about what articles you might be able to share with their readers. Recently, I've also been asked about what videos I could share. What follow-up items do you have available for distribution?

Article Writing:

What are key topics your clients want to hear about? What do they want resources around?

_____

_____

Identify 5 topics for each one.

_____   _____

_____   _____

_____   _____

_____   _____

_____   _____

Where do you want your articles to be found?

_____

_____

Research the publications related to your clients. What submission requirements do they have/need?

_____

_____

Strategy #6—Product Development

Product development provides a potential stream of revenue, and also offers a way for people to "get to know you" and benefit from your services in a different way. There are dozens of different products coaches can offer including:

- Journals
- Programs—bootcamps, group coaching, retreats (see the earlier on program development)
- Visual card decks
- Booklets
- White papers
- Workbooks

Related to the services you offer, what other products are your clients looking for? Make a list here.

_____

_____

_____

Strategy #7—Lunch and Learns

Another speaking strategy many coaches consider is offering lunch and learns to your target audience. Lunch and learns are typically short presentations (one hour or less) hosted by an organization or association, geared to provide their staff or members with "bite sized information". It's a great way to connect with potential clients, as well as get some immediate feedback on the topics and services you are offering. Lunch and learns are no longer just in-person events. Many professional organizations have moved to a virtual format.

If you're working with leaders, this is a great strategy and if you're doing something in wellness, lunch and learns may also be a great approach to building visibility. Lunch and learns also give you the opportunity to create a focus around the topics you are interested in.

What lunch and learn topics might you offer? Where?

_____

_____

Strategy #8—Associations

Associations can be a fantastic strategy to get in front of more corporate types of audiences. Regularly, associations are looking for conference speakers, lunchtime speakers, or dinner speakers. Connecting with professional associations are another way to start developing the conversation and relationship with prospective clients.

The great thing with associations and conferences is it can also be a mutual learning experience. If you are wanting to get connected with new niches, attending conferences can be educational in terms of discovering the key things and topics people are interested in. What are the conversations they are having? What can you add into that conversation space?

What associations might you reach out to?

_____

_____

Strategy #9—Trade Shows and Conferences

Trade shows and conferences are another strategy to incorporate in terms of building relationships, getting out there, and also seeing what's happening in your industry. While they can be costly to host a table/booth, they are a great way to build visibility in the long term. Having a clear budget and strategy is important.

What are you offering? This could be a collaborative initiative with other professionals. During my first few months of business I banded together with some other coaches in the Toronto area, and, over the course of two or three days offered what seemed like hundreds of Wheel of Life laser coaching sessions to people who dropped by our booth. I still attribute it to one of the best ways to practice and describe what coaching is, and what I do as a coach.

What trade shows might you explore attending, speaking at or being a vendor at?

_____

_____

Now over to you...Field Work

So, you've had a brain dump of ideas here. Now for some field work for you. The impact of coaching happens when we put it into action.

Take 15 minutes before moving on to think about two to three or more vehicles or strategies you want to employ in your business.

What could it look like if you were to put some attention around speaking? What would that mean in your world of work? Would it be booking a speaking engagement every month or booking one every week? Or do you want to do 50 in the next quarter?

It's up to you. Think about what's going to help you move forward and gain visibility as a business. It's important to not only put attention on what you want to do, but also put some focus on the content. In terms of planning it can be useful to capture your ideas on a MindMap (see the space provided in Section 5 in the Back Pages). I would encourage you to develop MindMaps around the topic areas you want to speak about, writing, blog about, or go to conferences around. It's really key that we have a clear line of sight on our message, as well as provide the messages that people are looking for.

If you're drawing a blank on what you might want to re-do yourself, take a look online. Do an index search on what people are writing, speaking, blogging, meeting about—you'll get some good data.

Once you have captured your ideas, also take a few minutes to complete the following chart, noting the pros and cons for yourself of the different promotional strategies, and what they could look like specifically for your business.

Strategy	Pros	Cons	What it could look like for me
1—Speaking			
2—Blogging			
3—Podcasting			
4—Networking			
5—Article Writing			
6—Product Development			
7—Lunch and Learns			
8—Associations			
9—Trade Shows and Conferences			

Building Visibility—Web and Online Presence

I've separated out this visibility tip for web and online presence to make the distinction that having a website is not the same as having an online presence.

In addition to having your own company website or program-specific websites, you will want to develop an online presence. This may be a combination of a LinkedIn page, a Facebook page, an Instagram account and a Twitter feed that directs to blog posts you've written or photos you've taken.

Having a web presence is key. Web presence is wider than a website. Whether you are using your website as a virtual calling card or whether you're creating something more interactive, be aware that your "digital footprint" can become quite pronounced. We want this to be shaped by who our clients are, and their preferences. Our preferences are also important to consider as building visibility is an ongoing activity. If we commit to doing things that we don't enjoy it's unlikely that we will sustain it.

Now there are multiple platforms you can choose from in starting to build a web presence. Are you creating a Facebook landing page, or a blog site where there's a blog embedded, or perhaps a WordPress site?

What is the purpose of the website? Is it to:

Inquiry: What is the starting place for web presence for you? What is important about having a web presence?

- let people know about what you have to offer,
- host your blog
- provide course information and announcements
- accept registrations
- other?

I continue to meet coaches who spend six to nine to twelve months getting their website perfected. Many times, once it's done, their focus may have shifted, or they might need to update different services they are offering.

What is important for you as you think about your website or web presence?

_____

_____

Ultimately, coaches can put themselves in a financially pressurized position because they're not bringing revenue in the door. The "**good enough**" mindset may be an appropriate strategy when it comes to website development.

There continues to be debate around pricing and web presence. Personally, I include my pricing on my website. It's a business philosophy. I want to be very transparent. I also don't want to be spending a lot of time going through how much does this cost and what does it include. It's right there for people to review before they make the buying decision. This is not the same philosophy which other businesses coaches hold. Again, you'll want to think about what is important for you and your business. How many clients do you have *over* the course of the year and what makes sense for letting them know what you have to offer?

Driving Traffic to Your Site

Having a website is not enough. It's imperative that you drive traffic to your site. Otherwise, you may have spent a lot of effort in designing a work of art, which no one knows about.

In driving traffic to your site think about promotion. You will want to make sure that people know about your website, so think about how you can incorporate mention of it — in your signature line on email, add a mention to the footer of your blog posts as a link; mention it in audio posts that you're doing; and if you're on social media (i.e., Facebook or Twitter) make mention of your site to help drive traffic there.

Finding an Accountability Partner

The old saying goes, "no man is an island," or as I like to say, in a more gender-inclusive language, "no person can do it alone."

This section gets you to think about accountability partners and developing a series or a network of people who can support you in your work. Regardless of what stage of business we are in, having accountability partners is key.

While I've named this tip accountability partners, these tips can apply to any partnership. In fact, many of us have multiple joint ventures or partnerships.

Some of the most enjoyable work that I do is with colleagues. The work can range from bringing people onboard as a sub-contractor for larger engagements that I'm responsible for, to actually developing joint programs and running it under shared banners. Consider viewing partnerships in a wider lens.

As new and experienced business owners, if we're running virtual work, it can be very isolating. Therefore, it can be really useful to have a variety of professionals to tap into, and a variety of relationships to leverage— from collaborators, to peers, to mentors.

It is quite common, I think for coaches of all maturities, in terms of our business timeline, to have accountability partners around us. These are people who will help us, cheerlead us on, help us move through the ups and downs, the peaks and valleys of a business, and, sometimes, round us out.

So, who's going to help you, round you, challenge you, and also support you in thinking and acting in different ways?

_____

_____

Resources: Download a Digital chapter on Co-Facilitation at https://www.from12many.com/downloads.html (Use code 4411).

Also use the Content Collaboration Planner in Section 5 to highlight others you want to partner with around content. You might partner with them by guest blogging, or being a podcast guest, or holding a joint venture.

Co-facilitation is an important partnership that you might want to be develop, so rather than have you invent the wheel, I will invite you to download the chapter and review best practices around co-facilitation.

Thinking about yourself:

What does partnership mean in your world?

_____

_____

Is it an accountability partner that you want to create?

_____

_____

Is it developing a network of co-facilitators that you can work with? What might that look like?

_____

_____

Phases of the Co-Facilitation Journey:

Masterful co-facilitation and partnering doesn't just happen. It takes work and usually multiple conversations. In my most recent book, Effective Virtual Conversations, I share the following questions to be asking, and areas to be exploring, at all phases of the co-facilitation or partnering journey. Consider bringing these into your conversations.

At the Start:
- What are our strengths?
- How are we complimentary?
- Where do gaps exist?
- What blindspots do we have?
- What is important in our work? What values drive our work?
- What business philosophies are important to us?
- Share samples of work

During Design:
- Who will take a lead on what?—Design and Facilitation
- Accordion points—what can be expanded and needs to be contracted if needed
- What is our common stake for this program?
- What do we want to ensure happens, no matter what?

During Implementation:
- Review leads for each section
- Observations with group—energy, impact, engagement
- Add additional questions
- Accordion
- Touch base throughout regarding changes needed

Post Program:
- Review of program—What worked well? What didn't?
- Successes
- Roles, flow and fit
- Lessons learned
- Changes for next co-facilitation

Source: Effective Virtual Conversations, Jennifer Britton, page 390, 2017.

Activity: What are the questions you want to ask or conversations you want to have at the different stages of the partnership journey?

At the Start:	During Design:

During Implementation:	Post Program:

Social Proof and Other Testimonials

Harnessing the great results you have had is a key part of social proof and other testimonials. Social proof in today's world is so key and it's irregular. It's a newer term that we're using these days to talk about testimonials. It's about letting the world know about the successes you and your clients have had. As coaches it is important to keep in mind the confidentiality agreement within the coaching relationship. Have your past clients given you approval to name them as past clients? That's something you'll definitely have to talk about.

Some of us are bound by nondisclosure agreements, so we can never use the name of the companies we work for.

We may, however, be able to create some case studies without using names. I think an important part of creating undeniable value is making sure that your work does have undeniable value.

So, it is important to evaluate your programming and services at multiple touch points. I like to evaluate midpoint, and at the end-point, of any process or program. Usually that means the three-month mark and six-month mark.

Part of social proof is to track your past clients short-term, as well as in the medium-term and long-term. Case studies can bring to life people's experience, whether it's organizational case studies or even a case study of a business owner you worked with. Areas you might include in a case study are:

- What was the process you employed?
- What were the benefits?
- What were some of the key learnings?

I'll invite you to think about how you can capture social proof. How can you capture the value that you bring?

_____

_____

What is the value that you bring? We need to be asking our clients about the value they have derived from our work. Nothing is more powerful than using their voice through testimonials. Video is a whole new way that we can capture testimonials in addition to having them write something.

What can you do to capture the success stories that you've had with clients before moving on?

Evaluation in your program is also important.

- What have you heard about the successes of your clients?
- What have they found valuable?
- What specifically would you like to demonstrate or showcase around social proof?

What evaluation feedback can you capture going forward?

_____

_____

What social proof would you like to harness?

_____

_____

What case studies can you create?

_____

_____

_____

End-of-Section Checkpoint

What are the key items you want to remember from this section?

_____

_____

What do you want to add to your plans?

_____

_____

What has become really clear for you so far?

_____

_____

_____

_____

Section 4

The Ecosystem

This section turns attention to your own internal ecosystem, and yourself as a business owner. The section invites you to consider what is important for you to consider on an individual level. In tandem with this section, consider what you want to add to your plans, including your One Page Plan.

Business Vision

"To the person who does not know where he wants to go there is no favorable wind." –Seneca

Why Business Vision is Important:

As I wrote earlier, having a business vision helps us through the ebbs and flows of business. It also creates a compelling focus to move us through the ups and downs. Sometimes it's what we need to push us that much farther or create urgency around what we are doing.

Why are you starting, or growing, your business? What will it enable you to do?

As we step into the place of visioning, I would like to invite you to consider: What's possible for you? What's possible two years from now? Ten years from now?

By asking the question "What's possible?" we are activating the parts of the brain that comprise the Positive Emotional Attractor Network. This literally "opens up the brain" for exploration.

This section is going to support you in defining what your vision is for the upcoming year.

For taking notes on this next activity on vision, you are encouraged to use a blank piece of paper or use your journal.

You may even want to set a timer and dedicate 5-10 minutes to each question.

Spend the next period refining and detailing what you would like your work or your business to look like this time next year. Some of you might be using a slightly different planning process so you might be thinking about your business three or five years from now.

Thinking about your work, your business, your team:

1. [One year from now] what do you want your business to look like?
2. [One year from now] what are the major goals you, your team, and your organization or business have achieved?
3. What impact has your business or work had?
4. What impact has it had on you?
5. What impact has it had on others?
6. What do you know about the successes you've had?
7. What challenges have you been able to overcome?
8. Looking back a year from now, what are people saying about you?
9. What are people saying about your business or your organization and what are people saying about your team?
10. One year from now, what do you know about your biggest achievements?
11. How can you expand on these?
12. One year from now, who is on your team? What do they do? What do they bring?

13. What changes, if any, are needed to the team one year from now?

14. What is your total revenue? How much has come in the door in this past year or through the projects you manage? What have been the total sales?

15. What's possible in your work?

16. What are the main lines of your business?

17. What are those different components that make up your work? What's the blend?

18. What is the amount and type of work you are doing?

19. Think about a typical day—is it at the office? On the road? Doing what?

20. What's working really, really well?

21. What's not working so well?

22. What are the areas you might want to make some changes in?

23. And finally, a year from now, what are you most excited about?

Take a few more minutes to further reflect on these questions and continue to develop and capture what your vision is for your business or your work over the coming year.

This is a monthly or quarterly activity you may want to schedule in. Take a moment to mark it in your quarterly and/or monthly plans using the templates in Section 5.

Who do you want to share this with? What can you do to keep this visible?

_____

_____

_____

_____

_____

_____

_____

_____

_____

_____

_____

_____

_____

_____

_____

Vision Timeline

Now that you have your vision timeline, I'd like you to start chunking it out into a timeline. What are you going to do when? Use this timeline sheet to do this.

Month	Key Activities

Checkpoint:

What has become really clear for you so far?

_____

_____

Second, what are you most excited about?

_____

_____

What is the one area for you to put some attention around right now?

_____

_____

Strengths

The next area of the ecosystem we are going to explore is strengths. Coaching is generally a strengths-based approach.

So, here's the business case for strengths. Gallup[18] found that employees who are encouraged to use their strengths by their managers:

- Are six times more engaged in their work
- Generate 8.9% greater profitability
- Report 12.5% greater productivity.

Even if you're not a numbers person, this is significant. Engagement is a crisis, or at least a key driver, across most organizations today, unless you work in one of those exceptional businesses. This is where I help small business truly up the ante in terms of engagement.

If you're a leader of a team or an owner of a business, we want to be inviting people to bring their best selves to work every day.

So, this activity is geared to get you to understand what your strengths are and to have a deeper appreciation of how you're going to be able to use them EVERY day.

I've had the opportunity over the last decade to work with many teams across a wide variety of industries—healthcare, financial services, education. Strengths coaching has been significant in boosting connection, collaboration, and understanding amongst the team members. There are three main strengths assessments, including the third one listed here that will be an interest for those who are entrepreneurs or small-business owners.

---

18 http://news.gallup.com/businessjournal/155036/embedding-strengths-company-dna.aspx

Part 1—Complete one of the strengths assessments that are available.

#1: The VIA Strengths Assessment (http://www.viacharacter.org/) which emerged out of the positive positive psychology movement. There are millions of people who have completed the strength assessment online over the last decade.

#2: The StrengthsFinder2.0—The second assessment comes from Gallup. Many of you might have already completed it. If you have, pull out your strengths finder report.

#3: The Entrepreneurial StrengthsFinder. In 2014, there was the launch of the Entrepreneurial StrengthsFinder, specific to the world of the entrepreneur. If you are a business owner, this might be the one that you want to go with.

To explore strengths you might choose a couple of options depending on your budget and your time. Complete the survey of your choice and review the report that is generated.

Part 2—Exploring with your top five strengths.

In the space below, write down the answers to these questions about your strengths—as identified by the report.

Questions:

1. What are your top five strengths? List them.
2. What does each strength mean? Look like in action?
3. What is this strength all about?
4. Where and when do you use it?
5. What impact does it have?
6. What does the strength look like under stress and pressure?

Strength:

Strength:

Strength:

Strength:

Strength:

Research continues to show employees who are able to use their strengths on a regular basis are much more productive and positive.

Resources-Strengths:

StrengthsFinder 2.0

Strengths Based Leadership by Barry Conchie and Tom Rath, which was published in 2009 by Gallup.

Now, Discover Your Strengths, was published in 2001 by Marcus Buckingham and, of course, Donald Clifton who was the designer of the original StrengthsFinder.

Buckingham followed up in 2010 with *Go Put Your Strengths to Work.*

I also recommend the free online assessment—VIA is VIA Survey of Character Strengths which comes out of the Positive Psychology movement.

In closing, now that you've undertaken your activity:

What do you need to add to your plans?

_____

_____

As you review these, how aligned are they with your clients and their needs?

_____

_____

What's important to remember about what you've discovered about strengths?

_____

_____

And finally, how are your strengths reflected in your goals?

_____

_____

THE SWOT—Looking at Your Inner and Outer Context

For many years I've introduced the SWOT tool to hundreds of business owners, leaders, and team members. I'm always amazed at how this framework sparks a conversation. The SWOT is a strategic planning tool that has been around for decades. It helps us explore and understand the context in which we operate.

The SWOT helps us get a lay of the land—by looking at our strengths, our weaknesses, our opportunities, and threats. It gives us a picture of the internal and external context we are facing.

As a starting point in the SWOT, we are going to first look at our internal context—or what is internal to the organization and in our control. As you look at the SWOT framework, the strengths and weaknesses are those things that are internal to us as individuals or organizations.

For example, a strength may be verbal communication, technical skills or our team.

I'd like you to pause for a couple of minutes and I'd like you to take stock, take inventory of all those things you do really well as an individual leader or as a business. Write these in the strengths box which follows.

Next, what are the weaknesses you have as a business (or business owner)? What are those areas that do get in a way? What are those areas that need attention? Our weaknesses have the potential to bring the organization down.

Weaknesses might include organizational skills, lack of communication between departments, or lack of systems.

Take a minute to pause and write these in your own worksheet:

Strengths	Weakness(es)

Take another look at the strengths and weaknesses that you just identified. As you look at your strengths, put a check mark beside the ones that are your greatest assets. *What are the things that, if you did more of, would really make a difference in your work?*

NOW, looking at the weaknesses, put a star beside the ones that might have the potential to really get in the way. *What can you do to mitigate against these?*

Next, we are going to move on to the external environment, which focuses on identifying opportunities and threats. These are the things that are outside of us, outside of our leadership, outside of our organization.

Opportunities may represent new business contacts, changes in legislation that work for you (for example, less tax or mandated purchasing). Perhaps there's a currency change that works in your favor. Opportunities might include new collaborations or partners in a new area, or funding for an intern. What are the opportunities in your external business context?

Using the table below highlight your opportunities, those good things in the external environment that are happening. What resources, people, or situations can help you move forward? You will want to think about new projects, new legislation, or things that are happening in your environment.

Threats are other external forces that might pose a threat to your business or yourself. A threat could include things like government taxes, new competitors, changes to global tariffs, new competitors moving into your area or space.

What are the resources, people, or situations that could derail your plan? Again, these are threats made by projects that are not going well. This might be things that are happening in the environment, new legislation, or competitors. What are the things that could potentially derail your business?

Opportunities	Threats

Now that you have your list, I'd like you to put a checkmark beside the top three opportunities you could pursue. We'll be exploring these more in-depth shortly.

Place a star beside the top three threats. What can you do to mitigate against them?

As a next step with this activity, you will want to transcribe these across to a full blown SWOT. In doing so, you might think about some new things. As we wrap up this section, what stands out? Is it your strengths, your weaknesses? What makes your business or work really unique? What can set you apart in the coming year?

Checkpoint: What do you need or what do you want to add to your plan? Before you move on to revisit your original vision, are there some things that you want to add to your plan or make a change? Also, revisit your one-page plan.

Bringing It All Together—The Ecosystem

We started this voyage by exploring each area separately—strengths, values, your SWOT, and your stance. You're now going to bring all these ideas together to represent the ecosystem. Just as in a rainforest, parts of the business that you create as the business owner are symbiotic and rely on each other. The roots, trunk, and branch are connected. They do not exist in isolation. In this module, we're going to be looking at your ecosystem—what makes you stand out.

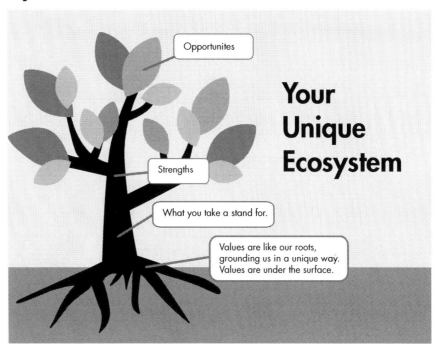

And as we'll see in this module—values, strengths, opportunities, threats—these create a unique ecosystem. I was originally trained as an ecologist and spent time living and working out of rainforests and cloud forests. Tropical rainforests include a series of symbiotic relationships that rely on one another. There are roots, leaves, and branches—in fact, in a rainforest what you realize is that much of life is patterned and integrated.

So, in this module we are going to be looking at your business ecosystem. In terms of who you are, let's start off by answering these questions:

What makes you stand out? What makes you unique? List out five things.

1. _____

2. _____

3. _____

4. _____

5. _____

In this section, we are going to be revisiting three areas that have preceded it: our values, our strengths, and our opportunities.

Values:

Values are like our roots, grounding us. They are under the surface of the earth—not always seen but we know when they are disturbed. Flip back to the values exercise we did earlier in the Iceberg Activity of Section 1.

Let's start with our values, those things that are important to us personally and/or professionally. Just like roots, they live below the surface, keeping us grounded. They are also invisible to others, often not becoming visible until they get stepped on.

Growing out of our roots is the trunk and what you take a stand for. What are the things you will go to bat for? What are the things you will ensure happen? NO MATTER WHAT.

If you have values of quality and excellence you might take a stand as a business by "going above and beyond." Or, if you have a value of diversity, you might take a stand for offering your client a series of products and services, not just one thing. Perhaps you take a stand for equity and ensure that everyone is treated equally.

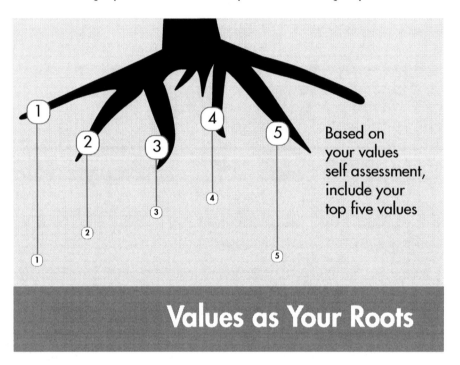

Based on your values self assessment, include your top five values

Values as Your Roots

Our Stance:

The tree trunk represents the things for which we take a stand. Take a moment and think about what plants your feet in the ground. As a coach, what do you do to ensure that people can do their best work possible? What is the stand you take for your customers? As a business?

What we take a stand is usually what we can be relied on for, or it might be a line we do not cross that helps us make decisions around focus, and priorities.

Like our values, what we take a stand for, often is illustrated in our actions. It may not be visible to everyone.

Take a few minutes writing down your values and how that reflects what you take a stand for:

Value	How it impacts what I take a stand for	My behaviors and how it shows up

The third area that we've explored recently are your strengths. In putting these into our ecosystem they are the branches. The branches are strong, and they really shape you as a professional.

Strengths:

Strengths are also like the branches—strong and shape you as a professional leader or business owner.

Note your top five strengths:

1. _____

2. _____

3. _____

4. _____

5. _____

Now turn to the Ecosystem worksheet and lay out these top five strengths in each of the five branches, first listing the strength. Then, one branch at a time, consider the questions:

When you use this strength, what's possible?

When you use this strength, what are you able to do, or accelerate, or create?

Do this for all five strengths and note what is possible. As soon as you have laid that out, stop and pause and take an overall view of the tree.

What is the connection across the tree?

What do you notice about what is possible as you look across the branches?

What is the sweet spot or point of intersection?

What can you do to leverage it?

Just a reminder, as we said when we are able to use our strengths every day, we are more positive, we are more productive, and we get more done!

Layering on Opportunities

Now, let's add on the layer of opportunities. As you look at the opportunities facing you, what is possible if you leverage each one?

As you think about this opportunity, what possibility/possibilities is it creating?

If you were to follow this opportunity, what is a quick win or low hanging fruit?

What would quickly get you some momentum?

What would an early success look like if you were to follow this opportunity?

Opportunities

List each of your top 5 opportunities. With each one consider these questions:

What's important about this? What can you do to leverage your values and strengths? What would a quick win look like?

Opportunity	Reflections

Once you have completed your "deep dive" into opportunity #1, work on the other opportunities you have identified. Each time consider these questions and write down your responses to:

1.   What is the opportunity?

2.   What's important about it?

3.   What are the quick wins, or low hanging fruit?

4.   How does this opportunity leverage your values and strengths?

5.   One year in the future, what would your business look like if this opportunity came to fruition?

The Ecosystem is a living, breathing space, and just like in nature, our context internally and externally is always changing. I would invite you to revisit this regularly throughout the year, perhaps as part of a quarterly review. Notice what changes, and what stays the same. Likely, your values and strengths will become even more present, and your opportunities may shift a little bit.

As we wrap up, what is the connection between your opportunities? What is the connection between your strength and your roots? Think about your own unique ecosystem.

What have you discovered about your own ecosystem?

_____

_____

What's important about what you discovered to take forward?

_____

_____

Who do you want to share this with?

_____

_____

I encourage you to take a few minutes to pause and think of how this connects with your plan, where are you getting most excited? What feels a bit challenging?

Even as we think of opportunities, something that occurs during the process of change is the upset of the status quo. One thing that might get activated is our INNER Critic, often known in some coaching models as the Saboteur. This inner critic may be the voice saying, "You can't do that" or "You are not good enough." Rick Carson writes about working with this same voice that he names the Gremlin. This voice can be a powerful force against the process of change. It can make the change process more emotional.

Certainly, those of us who work in the area of coaching and development understand that one of the things that happens through change is "the activation of" the inner critic—those little voices that start speaking up and saying you can't do it. Some of you might be in that place. Although these are all great opportunities, change and progress are not always a natural evolution. Consider what you need and who you need for accountability and to get there.

In the Spotlight—Coaching Tool

An antidote to the voice of the Gremlin or Saboteur can be working through what is going to shift as you move through the process of change, identifying the enabling and constraining factors. One of my favorite tools to do this is the Force Field Analysis tool from Kurt Lewin. Let's use this tool to work through one of the changes you are facing in your business right now

The change I am facing:	
Enabling Forces	Restraining Forces

As we wrap up this section, what are the connections?

_____

_____

What have you discovered about your own ecosystem?

_____

_____

What implication(s) does this have for your plan and your business in the next year?

_____

_____

Where are you getting the most excited about right now and where do you feel the most challenged?

_____

_____

Keys for Business Success

Getting Into Action

We are what we repeatedly do. Excellence, therefore, is not an act but a habit. –Wil Durant[19]

Action is key to any business success. In this module, we're going to look at four main areas. We're going to look at what it means to focus, to experiment, to create momentum, and, to celebrate.

Throughout the planner so far, we explored your unique ecosystem, your values, what you uniquely take a stand for, the strengths that you bring to the table as a leader or business owner, and your opportunities.

As we step into this section you might want to complete this quick activity. Go back to your vision and activity timeline. With the ecosystem we have just worked through consider what it means to get into action. I'd like you to think about what is really unique and where you might want to leverage. Does that make a shift to any of your one-page action plans? Pause and take five minutes to review your ecosystem and related action plans.

Once you've done that, return here as we look at Focus, Experimentation, Momentum and Celebration.

Focus

"People think focus means saying yes to the thing you've got to focus on, but that's not what it means at all. It means saying no to the hundred other good ideas that there are. You have to pick carefully." –Steve Jobs[20]

Another key part of business success is focus. As business owners, especially as solopreneurs, we cannot do it all. Focus is important as it helps to:

- Avoid dilution of what we are doing
- Create momentum
- Find balance

What else does focus provide for you?

As a business owner, I'm just as proud of the things I haven't done as the things I have done. Innovation is as much about saying NO as it is YES.

Without focus, we might dilute the important things in our work.

Activity: Take a look again at your vision and your activity timeline.

What are those things that you might want to say no to?

_____

_____

Chances are in today's world, you've got a long To-Do list and it's probably just as important to say no as it is to say yes.

---

19 https://medium.com/the-mission/my-favourite-quote-of-all-time-is-a-misattribution-66356f22843d
20 https://www.goodreads.com/quotes/629613-people-think-focus-means-saying-yes-to-the-thing-you-ve

So, questions for you to consider here:

What does focus mean to you?

_____

_____

What are the top three things you want to focus on in your business right now?

1. _____

2. _____

3. _____

What will help you focus on the important things you've identified?

_____

_____

What do you need to say no to? In saying no, we are freeing up space to focus on the things that are important. What are the things you want to keep in focus that are important?

_____

_____

Experimentation

"You don't learn to walk by following rules, you learn by doing and by falling over."—Richard Branson[21]

Let's talk a little bit about experimentation. Experimentation is critical, especially to those of us who are business owners. As I wrote a few months ago at the Teams365 blog,

"The rapid changes being required of us in today's business context are calling for a need for skills in multiple areas. From enhanced listening skills, to cultivating curiosity, from experimentation to open-mindedness, from problem solving to prioritization, these are skills we want to cultivate in all of our team members."

Josh Kaufman explains the Experimental Mindset as:
"When improving yourself or your business, it's often not clear what approach will create the intended result. That's where the Experimental Mindset comes in handy. Constant experimentation is the only way you can identify what will actually produce the result you desire. Often, the best (or only) way to learn things is to jump in and try. At the beginning, you may be over your head, but there's no faster way to learn what works." https://personalmba.com/

---

21 https://www.brainyquote.com/quotes/richard_branson_414117

In my work with teams the experimental mindset can look like:

- Putting shorter time windows on projects, with quicker checkpoints to see what is working, and what is not.
- Moving projects out of design phase and into beta more quickly so that pilots can be rolled out and/or early adopters can take the program for a test drive.
- Deciding what "good enough" looks like or what is the "minimal viable product"
- Looking at testing a couple of different strategies at the same time, with the notion that they might not be as fully developed as they have been in the past. Early results may inform what gets further developed and/or followed.

A few questions for you to think about:

What does experimentation look like for you?

_____

_____

What does experimentation mean in your work?

_____

_____

Where would adopting more of an experimental mindset be useful in your work right now?

_____

_____

Where might you try out two different strategies at once?

_____

_____

What is your time window for experimentation and review?

_____

_____

Where can experimentation support your work and your growth in the coming year?

_____

_____

Momentum

Success is like a lightning bolt. It'll strike you when you least expect it, and you just have to keep the momentum going. You have to strike when the iron is hot. So for me, I just kept striking and striking to polish out the sword that I was making.
—Michelle Phan[22]

In *Good to Great*, author Jim Collins writes about the flywheel. As a former rower I know that there is always a stage at which the energy takes over and the flywheel starts to create momentum by itself, creating more energy with less input.

This section is about momentum. *What will help you gain or continue momentum?* When things move into action, like a snowball, they create their own life.

One of the coaching challenges I often provide for people who are feeling stuck is to start developing a habit of sitting down and taking 15 minutes to start to move through a task or an activity.

That simple act in and of itself can create its own momentum.

So, think for yourself, what will help you gain or continue momentum?

_____

_____

What are those things that are going to help you gain and continue with momentum? Perhaps it's adding members to your team or perhaps it's scheduling off time.

_____

_____

Where do you want to build in "pause points" to recharge?

_____

_____

_____

_____

Pick up your calendar and schedule these in now. If you don't, it's unlikely you will have space to complete them. Think school holidays, March break, important days of the year, holiday seasons, and time off. If you are a parent, when do you also get a break?

High performance is as much of recharging and renewing as it is doing the work.

_____

22 https://www.brainyquote.com/quotes/michelle_phan_743716?src=t_momentum

Reflective Pauses and Celebration

"Life can only be understood backwards; but it must be lived forwards." –Søren Kierkegaard[23]

Creating pause points along the journey is important, and I hope that you have been able to dip into this workbook across time.

Part of scheduling reflection is also about scheduling celebration. In today's world it's easy to not stop to acknowledge what you have done.

What are you going to do to celebrate when you achieve your milestones?

_____

_____

What reflection points will you build in to pause and celebrate along the way?

_____

_____

It is my hope that you will take some time to schedule time to pause and recharge.

Time Management and Personal Productivity for the Business Owner

Doing more with less is a key mantra of today's business context. At the same time, most of us are inundated with email. Consider these factoids:

- 40% of our productivity can be lost due to multitasking or what's called task switching.[24]
- The Washington Post reported in late 2016 that we spend almost 20.5 hours a week looking at email.[25]

Time magazine has indicated that typical managers face up to 56 interruptions in the day.[26] Consider that number of interruptions in a day, maybe over the span of seven, eight, nine or ten hours. And, of course, we all know that information overwhelm continues to increase.

One of my favorite factoids around time management is from Elaine Beech, who noted that in 2007 a daily issue of the *New York Times* contained more information than the average person was likely to encounter in their lifetime during the seventeenth century.

Where are we today with the changes over the last decade that have continued to expedite or accelerate change and complexity?

Consider the changes in the last ten years—the launch of the iPad/iPhone, the introduction of smart devices. Think about what else is different for you today than a decade ago?

---

23 https://www.brainyquote.com/quotes/soren_kierkegaard_105030
24 https://www.psychologytoday.com/us/blog/brain-wise/201209/the-true-cost-multi-tasking
25 https://www.washingtonpost.com/news/the-intersect/wp/2016/10/03/how-many-hours-of-your-life-have-you-wasted-on-work-email-try-our-depressing-calculator/?utm_term=.bcc9941a6e9b
26 http://content.time.com/time/magazine/article/0,9171,995299,00.html

It is commonly stated that information is doubling every two years, so that for some university students what they are studying becomes obsolete even before they graduate. The world of work and communication has shifted dramatically in the last decade.

Key issues in time management for business owners are *how do we focus* AND *how do we delegate*? Also, how do we make sure that we remain at our prime and manage interruptions.

So, hopefully, these are some of the issues that you've been thinking about as you've been developing your vision and thinking about goals.

The issues of time, focus, interruptions, and delegation have implications for leaders and business owners. The constant barrage of information and communication, and the potential to quickly become overwhelmed with information, is a "hot topic" across most industries today.

How do we navigate in this? How do we ensure that we are most successful within the context that we operate within?

I want to share with you a couple of ideas:

#1—Figure Out Where Your Time Goes

The first step is to figure out where your time goes and one easy way to do this is through a Time Tracker. A lot of us think we know where we spend our time, when in fact it may not be as representative of where our time is really being spent.

As a coach, when I work with a lot of my clients around tracking their time I get them to notice where their time is going over the span of a week to notice where their time is going. You can quickly do this on a piece of paper, or electronically, and track your time in 15- or 30-minute increments on a 24-hour basis for a week or two.

Block everything and categorize it into different categories. If you commute, you might have a commuting time, meeting time, email, timeless staff, time with finance, reporting, relationship management, doing the business, speaking, or marketing.

At the end of a week, summarize, look back, and note at where your time ACTUALLY was spent. Reflect on these questions as you review the data:

First of all, what do you notice?

_____

_____

Where are you spending the bulk of your time?

_____

_____

What results are you getting from this?

_____

_____

What's not working?

_____

_____

What changes are needed to support you in maximizing your productivity and focus?

_____

_____

Where is your time really going?

_____

_____

If you're like me, tracking your time over a week is not going to be really representative of where time goes, but gives a starting point. I hear from my coaching clients that people are quite surprised by what they notice. *What's significant for you?*

#2—Prioritize Your Time

Number two is prioritize your time. As I wrote in the Teams365 back in 2015, *Priority comes from the Latin root of "prioritas," "prior" or former. It can be defined as "a thing that is regarded as more important than another."*

Throughout each business day we are prioritizing on individual and collective/team levels. Four prioritization tools you may find useful in your own work include:

Prioritization Tool #1: The Urgent/Important Matrix

Made famous by Steven Covey and his work, the Urgent/Important Matrix gets us to think about what is important and urgent in our work. Where are we spending our time? Are we focusing on things that are in the "crisis zone" of urgent and important, or are we able to be proactive and spend a bulk of our time in the not-urgent and important areas of planning, business building, and relationships?

Many professionals find themselves getting bogged down with the urgent and not important tasks— things like meetings that are not relevant, email, and reporting. And of course, the final part of the matrix is the land of the "time suckers" spending time in the not—urgent and not important tasks. The "time sucker" category includes excessive time spent on social media, back and forth emails that could be solved by a phone call, etc.

Activity: Think back to where you have spent your time over the last week. What quadrant are you spending the bulk of your time in? What's the impact of this?

Resource: Steven Covey—*Seven Habits of Highly Effective People*

Prioritization Tool #2: Prioritization Matrix

The prioritization matrix is a quick visual tool. What you will need is some post-it notes or a white board.

First, identify all of the priorities you have, writing each one down on a separate post-it.

Then rate them according to their impact and likelihood of getting them done (or other criterion).

Place them along the matrix of impact and likelihood.

This activity is very visual, and stimulates dialogue amongst the team members themselves. An important part of the prioritization process for teams is about sharing information, and also busting assumptions that might be held. This tool has the potential to be a great structure for facilitating that conversation.

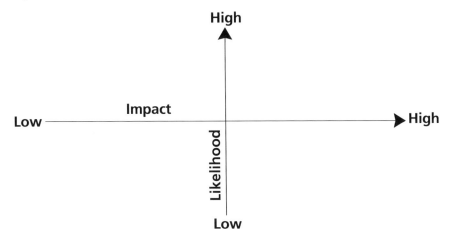

Prioritization Tool #3: 80/20 Rule

The Pareto principle, most commonly known as the 80/20 rule, another useful framework for prioritization. The 80/20 rule asserts that we get 80% of our results from 20% of our activities.

Business owners benefit from undertaking some analysis of where they are getting the bulk of their impact. This could include sales, key relationships, customer service, etc. Getting clear on these areas of impact will help us to prioritize them in the larger scheme of things.

Consider:

What is the 80% of your activities that are giving you your main results?

_____

_____

What is the 20% of your activities that are not yielding results?

_____

_____

What do you notice? What changes do you want to make?

_____

_____

Prioritization Tool #4: Strategic Issues Mapping

One of my favorite strategic prioritization tools I share with teams is Strategic Issues Mapping. This is an exercise to stimulate identification of issues, conversation, and sharing across a team, or by yourself, if you are a solopreneur.

Strategic issues mapping can be done on multiple levels. You might be looking at it from a short-term, medium-term and long-term perspective OR local, national and global.

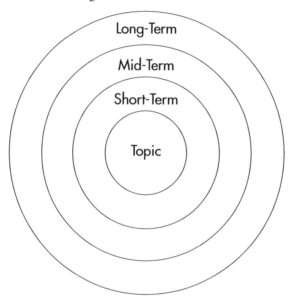

Start by putting the name of the issue you are exploring in the center of the circle. Next, have each team member brainstorm and write down all the issues/topics/challenges they can think of related to that topic. Next, label the surrounding circles according to short-term, medium-term and long-term issues OR label the issues according to impact (local, national, international).

One at a time, place the post-its in the relevant area. From this you may have dozens of issues.

As you complete your own Strategic Issues Map, what do you notice? Depending on time, you can explore multiple strategic issues you are facing, working circle by circle. As one of the starting points of these more focused explorations of each circle, I hand out colored dots to each participant and get them to dot the top two, three or more from their own perspective. This provides the team with a snapshot of where the collective sees the priorities, which can then feed into more dialogue, planning, and action.

These are only four prioritization tools out of myriad possibilities.

What prioritization tools and methods would be useful for you to use?

_____

_____

#3—Delegation

A third area important for time management is delegation. Delegation is critical for business owner success.

Taking a look at your priorities, ask yourself:

What do you really want to do?

_____

_____

What can only you do?

_____

_____

What could be handed off to others?

_____

_____

In starting to think about delegation and what we can delegate, we can apply the 5 Ws and an H to delegation:

1. **What**—What do you want to delegate? What are the specifics? What resources do they need to complete this?
2. **Who**—Who will you delegate to? Do they have the skills required? What support do they need along the way?
3. **When**—What are the major milestones along the way? How will you check in, and when?
4. **Why**—Why is this task important? Have you communicated the big picture?
5. **Where**—Where does the work need to take place?
6. **How**—What are the steps/actions required? How will it be measured? How will you all know it has been successful?

Tweetable Tip:
Do you fall into the trap of not delegating and doing it all yourself? At what cost?

A lot of leaders fall into the trap of not delegating and doing it all themselves. On the flipside, some leaders may over delegate, wondering why things are not done right. What is the cost of this? Often the questions flowing out of the 5 Ws have not been taken into account. Perhaps the person does not have the skills or resources to do the work, or maybe the authority to make it happen. Perhaps they've gotten things done, but there have been no checkpoints, so the actions taken really weren't the ones needed.

Coaching Questions:

- What do you want to delegate?
- Why is it important?
- Who can you delegate to?
- When will you check in?
- How do you find delegation as a skill set and practice yourself?

Task. Make a list of all the things you have to do this week or month. Check off ones that need to be done by you. Looking at what's left, what could you focus on?

Task	Done by me	Delegate	Defer to...	Delete

#4—Managing Interruptions

The fourth tip in prioritizing your time is about managing interruptions. As I said, the typical leaders can be interrupted up to 56 times a day. So, every time we do get interrupted, we need to stop what we're doing, we need to refocus and then we need to get back into action again.

Studies from Dr. Gloria Mark show that it can take upwards of 22 minutes to get back on task again[27].

We often don't factor the **cost of the start up** again, so we might not completely be able to totally get rid of interruptions. What we want to do is be able to manage them more effectively.

Here are a few options for managing interruptions:

- Minimize interruptions (i.e., keeping emails off)

---

27 http://news.gallup.com/businessjournal/23146/too-many-interruptions-work.aspx

- Log your time tracker
- Notice where you're really getting interrupted

Consider which ones are important, which ones might need to be managed.

A really common interruption today is the constant ping of emails coming in. Is that something that you can have some control over? Can you structure uninterrupted blocks of 30-50 minutes at a time by turning off your email for short periods?

A second tip or option for managing interruptions is to create a dedicated focus time. Can you leave the office or close the door, or do certain tasks when everyone has left the office, or during a day when you work from home?

Questions to consider:

Think about the different interruptions in your day, how do they happen? Is it email? Is it phone? Is it something else?

_____

_____

When do interruptions typically happen?

_____

_____

Where do interruptions happen?

_____

_____

What is possible for you to manage it?

_____

_____

End-of-Section Checkpoint

What are the key items you want to remember from this section?

_____

_____

What do you want to add to your plans?

_____

_____

What has become really clear for you so far?

_____

_____

_____

Putting It Into Action

"All good things must come to an end" is a phrase that's bandied around our home. While the text ends here, your work now begins. You'll notice that the rest of the workbook includes space for you to note your plans, tasks, and activities for the next 12 months.

Before you step into that, I want to remind you of where our journey has taken us. The first three sections explored business foundations, the Solopreneur Primer, along with marketing and promotional strategies.

As you moved through Section 4, you have really done a Herculean task of identifying your vision and looking at what is possible for you in the next year.

You'll recall we then moved into your vision roadmap and you identified the things that you would like to see happen in your own business or in your own work.

From there, we moved your vision forward by volumes, that big blank piece of paper that is now full.

We then moved into your activity roadmap where you broke out, month by month, key activities, resources required, and some of your end results you're going to be looking at.

From there we moved into the next section of the program, which was all about you, what makes you unique and your values. What are your individual values? What are your team, department, and organizational values? You came up with your top five values, and reflected on how you are leading with those every day.

We moved into our strengths and answered very similar questions around what makes you unique. What are the strengths that you uniquely bring to the table? Maybe you did the VIA Strengths Assessment. Some of you may have worked on looking at the StrengthsFinder or even the Entrepreneurial Strengths. No matter what assessment you chose, there were some questions there for you to reflect upon as you thought about your strengths.

We then moved to the context in which you operate—and looked at the SWOT because we do not operate in a vacuum. So, you explored what your strengths, weaknesses, opportunities, and threats are, and then put it all together. We also saw how the roots of a tree represent our values.

We determined what you take a stand for, your strengths, and, of course, your opportunities.

I really hope that this has been a great process for you to identify what is key for you. As we get into action and start putting things into practice it is important to keep in mind focus, experimentation, momentum, and celebration.

So, congratulations, you've got an initial plan in your hand!

Now, what will it take to make this happen no matter what?

I would invite you to share your accountability with those around you. What we do know anecdotally is that when public announcements are made around accountability that there is a greater chance that things will get done!

So, I eagerly encourage you to take some time to share this with your colleagues, with someone in your close network so that they can support you through it the next year.

For ongoing tips and ideas, stay connected with us through PotentialsRealized.com and CoachingBusinessBuilder.com. I hope that you might even drop in and join us at the Coaching Biz Growth Lab where we meet twice a month for learning, coaching, and TAKING ACTION on our business!

Thanks for joining me on this journey! I look forward to continuing the conversation—

Jennifer

 Email me at info@potentialsrealized.com

 Connect on Facebook at EffectiveGroupCoaching

 Connect on Twitter @jennbritton

 Connect on Instagram @jenn.britton

 www.CoachingBusinessBuilder.com

Check out the Coaching Biz Growth Lab™ for ongoing business development support in a group setting. www.CoachingBizGrowthLab.com.

Section 5

The Planner

This section of the planner includes annual, quarterly, monthly, and daily worksheets. The planner is undated so you can start using the planner at any time. In this section you will find the following:

Annual Planning Tools:

Annual Master List—Things to Do this Year

Annual Goals/Vision—Use this sheet to capture your key vision elements for the year, as well as core goals you have.

The Metaview Annual Goals and Milestones—Use this to highlight quarterly goals and milestones on an annual basis.

Annual Tracker—Use this to track key action steps or achievements on an annual basis.

Annual Project Calendar—Use this to track annual project ideas

> Is there something you wish you had and don't see here? Reach out to Jennifer at info@potentialsrealized.com and let her know. We will likely create more supplemental planner resources based on needs and inquiries

Quarterly Planning Tools (4 in total—label the quarter you are working on)

Quarterly To-Dos/Reflections

Quarterly Overview

Monthly Planning Tools—Undated so you can start at any time

A sample Monthly Tracker is included to give you an idea of how you might want to use the monthly trackers.

Monthly Start Page—Use this to capture additional ideas and notes, or just doodles!

Monthly Calendar—Each month has it's own undated calendar. Date it and use the left side bar to list some of your major tasks that month.

Monthly To-Dos—Task List: Use this to capture key tasks and items for the month ahead.

Monthly One-Page Planner—Use this as a one-page overview to the month, noting your goals, projects, key tasks and habits.

This Month in Focus —A one pager to keep key tasks and priorities in mind. It can be useful to schedule time each week to review and note your successes, enablers, derailers, lessons learned, and take time to plan for the next week.

Monthly Daily Tracker—Use this to track daily actions across the entire month, for example, when you exercise, post on social media, or sales made. Take a look at the sample provided. Note your key priorities at the bottom of the page to keep you focused.

Taking Stock—Monthly Reflection—Use this at the end of the month to capture your achievements, relationships, projects, etc.

Content Planner

Content Brainstorming—Taking 10–15 minutes to capture all your ideas around content—writing, speaking, blogging—can help to keep you moving. Use this page to note your ideas about content.

Content Planner—Annual Overview: Use this worksheet to highlight your content focus across the year.

Monthly Content Tracker—Use this to track the posts you get out and where you post them each month (12 are included).

Monthly Content Journal—One Line a Day—Use this to capture key notes or one sentence around your day and/or content for that day.

31-Day Challenge—31-Day Challenges are a fun way to create momentum for yourself in your business. Set up your own 31-Day Challenge for your clients or track your own 31-Day Challenge

Content Collaboration Plan—Use this page to capture your ideas around content collaboration (think about partnerships, Joint Ventures, writing for other sources). It's followed with space for you to note how you want to scale key content through repurposing and/or republishing.

Future Content Ideas—Use this for capturing more ideas about content.

The "Back Pages"—Creative Tools

Ideas for Next Time—Use this to capture lessons learned, and ideas for "next time"

Brainstorming Sheet—Use this as a place to brainstorm

Great Ideas to Action—Use as a space to list projects and ideas to put into action

The One Page Plan– This is probably the planning tool I talk about the most, and use most with coaching clients. Designed as a "one pager" which people can keep visible, the One Page Plan includes space to note your top five goals as well as detail around them, resources needed, timelines, and what's going to help and hinder the achievement of them.

Daily Planner
Download a copy of the daily planner for you to use at any time at www.CoachingBusinessBuilder.com/daily-planner

Annual Planning Tools

Annual Master List – Things To Do This Year

Annual Vision — 12 Months From Now

Financial Goals

Client Goals

Product/Program Goals

Lifestyle and Health Goals

Marketing Goals

Projects

Other Goals

Other Goals

Metaview Annual Goals and Milestones

	January	February	March
Quarter 1			

	April	May	June
Quarter 2			

	July	August	September
Quarter 3			

	October	November	December
Quarter 4			

Annual Tracker

Q1	January	February	March
Q2	April	May	June
Q3	July	August	September
Q4	October	November	December

Annual Project Calendar

January	February	March
April	May	June
July	August	September
October	November	December

Quarterly Planning Tools

Quarterly To-Dos

1 2 3 4 Quarter

Quarterly Reflections

Projects	Achievements	Learning	Opportunities	Other

Quarterly Planner

1 2 3 4 Quarter

Month	
Week 1	
Week 2	
Week 3	
Week 4	
Week 5	
Month	
Week 1	
Week 2	
Week 3	
Week 4	
Week 5	
Month	
Week 1	
Week 2	
Week 3	
Week 4	
Week 5	

Projects

Top 5 Goals

1.

2.

3.

4.

5.

Notes

Quarterly To-Dos

Quarterly Reflections

Projects	Achievements	Learning	Opportunities	Other

Quarterly Planner

1 2 3 4 Quarter

Month	
Week 1	
Week 2	
Week 3	
Week 4	
Week 5	
Month	
Week 1	
Week 2	
Week 3	
Week 4	
Week 5	
Month	
Week 1	
Week 2	
Week 3	
Week 4	
Week 5	

Projects

Top 5 Goals

1.

2.

3.

4.

5.

Notes

Quarterly To-Dos

1 2 3 4 Quarter

Quarterly Reflections

Projects	Achievements	Learning	Opportunities	Other

Quarterly Planner

1 2 3 4 Quarter

Month	
Week 1	
Week 2	
Week 3	
Week 4	
Week 5	
Month	
Week 1	
Week 2	
Week 3	
Week 4	
Week 5	
Month	
Week 1	
Week 2	
Week 3	
Week 4	
Week 5	

Projects

Top 5 Goals

1.

2.

3.

4.

5.

Notes

Quarterly To-Dos

1 2 3 4 Quarter

Quarterly Reflections

Projects	Achievements	Learning	Opportunities	Other

Quarterly Planner

1 2 3 4 Quarter

Month	
Week 1	
Week 2	
Week 3	
Week 4	
Week 5	
Month	
Week 1	
Week 2	
Week 3	
Week 4	
Week 5	
Month	
Week 1	
Week 2	
Week 3	
Week 4	
Week 5	

Projects

Top 5 Goals

1.

2.

3.

4.

5.

Notes

Open Space – Ideas/Musings/Jottings

Monthly Planning Tools

Monthly Daily Tracker

Month of _____

Day	Sales	Calls	Exercise	Writing	Network	FB	LI	Twitter	Speak	Other	
1	500	4	▓						▓		
2		5	▓								
3	500	5	▓			▓	▓	▓			
4		2	▓								
5	1000	5		▓	▓						
6											
7											
8			▓								
9		2	▓								
10		5	▓								
11		6	▓								
12	40			▓							
13						▓	▓	▓			
14											
15	400	5	▓						▓		
16		6									
17		2									
18		4									
19		6		▓							
20	100										
21											
22			▓								
23		2	▓								
24			▓								
25		5	▓								
26											
27	80										
28											
29											
30											
31											

SAMPLE LEGEND

You can choose your own areas to track

Sales: Amount of daily sales in dollars
Calls: Number of coaching calls or sales calls
Exercise: Any physical excercise
Writing:
Networking:
FB: Facebook
LI: LinkedIn
Twitter
Other: Any other tasks you want to track

Top Priorities

Notes

Monthly Plan for

_____

Monthly Calendar

Sunday	Monday	Tuesday	Wednesday

Month of _____

Thursday	Friday	Saturday	Notes

Month of
_____

Monthly To-Dos

Theme:

Top Goals:

Monthly One-Page Planner

Month of
_____

Top 5 Goals This Month

Goals

Financial Goals:

Marketing Goals:

Relationship Goals:

Monthly To-Dos:

Projects

Projects TO START this month:

Projects TO COMPLETE this month:

Projects TO CONTINUE this month:

Key Tasks for the Week of:

Week 1	Week 2	Week 3	Week 4	Week 5

Key Habits to Lean into:

This month will be a wild success when:

The Month in Focus

	Week 1	Week 2	Week 3	Week 4
Key Priorities				
Key Successes				
Enablers				
Derailers				
Lessons Learned				
Next week I will…				

Monthly Daily Tracker

Month of _____

Day										
1										
2										
3										
4										
5										
6										
7										
8										
9										
10										
11										
12										
13										
14										
15										
16										
17										
18										
19										
20										
21										
22										
23										
24										
25										
26										
27										
28										
29										
30										
31										

Top Priorities

Notes

Taking Stock – Monthly Reflections

Month of
_____

Achievements:

Key Metrics (Finances/Numbers)

Income:

Expenses:

Social Media:

Marketing:

Other:

What worked this month:

What didn't:

Opportunities:

Obstacles:

Key Learning:

Relationships

Who helped me:

Relationships I need to cultivate:

Relationships that need attention:

Projects

Completed:

Still in process:

New/On Horizon:

Looking Ahead to the Next Month

Lessons learned and changes:

What I want to do to support my vision:

Top priorities:

Monthly Plan for

_____

Monthly Calendar

Sunday	Monday	Tuesday	Wednesday

Month of _____

Thursday	Friday	Saturday	Notes

Month of

Monthly To-Dos

Theme:

Top Goals:

Monthly One-Page Planner

Month of
_____

Top 5 Goals This Month

Goals

Financial Goals:

Marketing Goals:

Relationship Goals:

Monthly To-Dos:

Projects

Projects TO START this month:

Projects TO COMPLETE this month:

Projects TO CONTINUE this month:

Key Tasks for the Week of:

Week 1	Week 2	Week 3	Week 4	Week 5

Key Habits to Lean into:

This month will be a wild success when:

The Month in Focus

Month of
_____

	Week 1	Week 2	Week 3	Week 4
Key Priorities				
Key Successes				
Enablers				
Derailers				
Lessons Learned				
Next week I will...				

Monthly Daily Tracker

Month of _____

Day											
1											
2											
3											
4											
5											
6											
7											
8											
9											
10											
11											
12											
13											
14											
15											
16											
17											
18											
19											
20											
21											
22											
23											
24											
25											
26											
27											
28											
29											
30											
31											

Top Priorities

Notes

Taking Stock – Monthly Reflections

Month of
_____

Achievements:

Key Metrics (Finances/Numbers)

Income:

Expenses:

Social Media:

Marketing:

Other:

What worked this month:

What didn't:

Opportunities:

Obstacles:

Key Learning:

Relationships

Who helped me:

Relationships I need to cultivate:

Relationships that need attention:

Projects

Completed:

Still in process:

New/On Horizon:

Looking Ahead to the Next Month

Lessons learned and changes:

What I want to do to support my vision:

Top priorities:

Monthly Plan for

_____

Monthly Calendar

Sunday	Monday	Tuesday	Wednesday

Month of _____

Thursday	Friday	Saturday	Notes

Month of
_____

Monthly To-Dos

Theme:

Top Goals:

Monthly One-Page Planner

Month of
_____

Top 5 Goals This Month

Goals

Financial Goals:

Marketing Goals:

Relationship Goals:

Monthly To-Dos:

Projects

Projects TO START this month:

Projects TO COMPLETE this month:

Projects TO CONTINUE this month:

Key Tasks for the Week of:

Week 1	Week 2	Week 3	Week 4	Week 5

Key Habits to Lean into:

This month will be a wild success when:

The Month in Focus

Month of
_____

	Week 1	Week 2	Week 3	Week 4
Key Priorities				
Key Successes				
Enablers				
Derailers				
Lessons Learned				
Next week I will…				

Monthly Daily Tracker

Month of _____

Day										
1										
2										
3										
4										
5										
6										
7										
8										
9										
10										
11										
12										
13										
14										
15										
16										
17										
18										
19										
20										
21										
22										
23										
24										
25										
26										
27										
28										
29										
30										
31										

Top Priorities

Notes

Taking Stock – Monthly Reflections

Month of
_____

Achievements:

Key Metrics (Finances/Numbers)

Income:

Expenses:

Social Media:

Marketing:

Other:

What worked this month:

What didn't:

Opportunities:

Obstacles:

Key Learning:

Relationships

Who helped me:

Relationships I need to cultivate:

Relationships that need attention:

Projects

Completed:

Still in process:

New/On Horizon:

Looking Ahead to the Next Month

Lessons learned and changes:

What I want to do to support my vision:

Top priorities:

Monthly Plan for

_____

Monthly Calendar

Sunday	Monday	Tuesday	Wednesday

Month of _____

Thursday	Friday	Saturday	Notes

Month of

_____

Monthly To-Dos

Theme:

Top Goals:

Monthly One-Page Planner

Month of

Top 5 Goals This Month

Goals

Financial Goals:

Marketing Goals:

Relationship Goals:

Monthly To-Dos:

Projects

Projects TO START this month:

Projects TO COMPLETE this month:

Projects TO CONTINUE this month:

Key Tasks for the Week of:

Week 1	Week 2	Week 3	Week 4	Week 5

Key Habits to Lean into:

This month will be a wild success when:

The Month in Focus

Month of
_____

	Week 1	Week 2	Week 3	Week 4
Key Priorities				
Key Successes				
Enablers				
Derailers				
Lessons Learned				
Next week I will…				

Monthly Daily Tracker

Month of _____

Day											
1											
2											
3											
4											
5											
6											
7											
8											
9											
10											
11											
12											
13											
14											
15											
16											
17											
18											
19											
20											
21											
22											
23											
24											
25											
26											
27											
28											
29											
30											
31											

Top Priorities

Notes

Taking Stock — Monthly Reflections

Month of

_____

Achievements:

Key Metrics (Finances/Numbers)

Income:

Expenses:

Social Media:

Marketing:

Other:

What worked this month:

What didn't:

Opportunities:

Obstacles:

Key Learning:

Relationships

Who helped me:

Relationships I need to cultivate:

Relationships that need attention:

Projects

Completed:

Still in process:

New/On Horizon:

Looking Ahead to the Next Month

Lessons learned and changes:

What I want to do to support my vision:

Top priorities:

Monthly Plan for

_____

Monthly Calendar

Sunday	Monday	Tuesday	Wednesday

Month of _____

Thursday	Friday	Saturday	Notes

Month of
_____

Monthly To-Dos

Theme:

Top Goals:

Monthly One-Page Planner

Month of

Top 5 Goals This Month

Goals

Financial Goals:

Marketing Goals:

Relationship Goals:

Monthly To-Dos:

Projects

Projects TO START this month:

Projects TO COMPLETE this month:

Projects TO CONTINUE this month:

Key Tasks for the Week of:

Week 1	Week 2	Week 3	Week 4	Week 5

Key Habits to Lean into:

This month will be a wild success when:

The Month in Focus

Month of
_____

	Week 1	Week 2	Week 3	Week 4
Key Priorities				
Key Successes				
Enablers				
Derailers				
Lessons Learned				
Next week I will…				

Monthly Daily Tracker

Month of _____

Day											
1											
2											
3											
4											
5											
6											
7											
8											
9											
10											
11											
12											
13											
14											
15											
16											
17											
18											
19											
20											
21											
22											
23											
24											
25											
26											
27											
28											
29											
30											
31											

Top Priorities

Notes

Taking Stock – Monthly Reflections

Month of
_____

Achievements:

Key Metrics (Finances/Numbers)

Income:

Expenses:

Social Media:

Marketing:

Other:

What worked this month:

What didn't:

Opportunities:

Obstacles:

Key Learning:

Relationships

Who helped me:

Relationships I need to cultivate:

Relationships that need attention:

Projects

Completed:

Still in process:

New/On Horizon:

Looking Ahead to the Next Month

Lessons learned and changes:

What I want to do to support my vision:

Top priorities:

Monthly Plan for

_____

Monthly Calendar

Sunday	Monday	Tuesday	Wednesday

Month of _____

Thursday	Friday	Saturday	Notes

Month of
_____

Monthly To-Dos

Theme:

Top Goals:

Monthly One-Page Planner

Month of
_____

Top 5 Goals This Month

Goals

Financial Goals:

Marketing Goals:

Relationship Goals:

Monthly To-Dos:

Projects

Projects TO START this month:

Projects TO COMPLETE this month:

Projects TO CONTINUE this month:

Key Tasks for the Week of:

Week 1	Week 2	Week 3	Week 4	Week 5

Key Habits to Lean into:

This month will be a wild success when:

The Month in Focus

Month of _____

	Week 1	Week 2	Week 3	Week 4
Key Priorities				
Key Successes				
Enablers				
Derailers				
Lessons Learned				
Next week I will...				

Monthly Daily Tracker

Month of _____

Day											
1											
2											
3											
4											
5											
6											
7											
8											
9											
10											
11											
12											
13											
14											
15											
16											
17											
18											
19											
20											
21											
22											
23											
24											
25											
26											
27											
28											
29											
30											
31											

Top Priorities

Notes

Taking Stock — Monthly Reflections

Month of
_____

Achievements:

Key Metrics (Finances/Numbers)

Income:

Expenses:

Social Media:

Marketing:

Other:

What worked this month:

What didn't:

Opportunities:

Obstacles:

Key Learning:

Relationships

Who helped me:

Relationships I need to cultivate:

Relationships that need attention:

Projects

Completed:

Still in process:

New/On Horizon:

Looking Ahead to the Next Month

Lessons learned and changes:

What I want to do to support my vision:

Top priorities:

Monthly Plan for

_____

Monthly Calendar

Sunday	Monday	Tuesday	Wednesday

Month of _____

Thursday	Friday	Saturday	Notes

Month of

Monthly To-Dos

Theme:

Top Goals:

Monthly One-Page Planner

Month of
_____

Top 5 Goals This Month

Goals

Financial Goals:

Marketing Goals:

Relationship Goals:

Monthly To-Dos:

Projects

Projects TO START this month:

Projects TO COMPLETE this month:

Projects TO CONTINUE this month:

Key Tasks for the Week of:

Week 1	Week 2	Week 3	Week 4	Week 5

Key Habits to Lean into:

This month will be a wild success when:

The Month in Focus

Month of
_____

	Week 1	Week 2	Week 3	Week 4
Key Priorities				
Key Successes				
Enablers				
Derailers				
Lessons Learned				
Next week I will…				

Monthly Daily Tracker

Month of _____

Day										
1										
2										
3										
4										
5										
6										
7										
8										
9										
10										
11										
12										
13										
14										
15										
16										
17										
18										
19										
20										
21										
22										
23										
24										
25										
26										
27										
28										
29										
30										
31										

Top Priorities

Notes

Taking Stock — Monthly Reflections

Month of
_____

Achievements:

Key Metrics (Finances/Numbers)

Income:

Expenses:

Social Media:

Marketing:

Other:

What worked this month:

What didn't:

Opportunities:

Obstacles:

Key Learning:

Relationships

Who helped me:

Relationships I need to cultivate:

Relationships that need attention:

Projects

Completed:

Still in process:

New/On Horizon:

Looking Ahead to the Next Month

Lessons learned and changes:

What I want to do to support my vision:

Top priorities:

Monthly Plan for

_____

Monthly Calendar

Sunday	Monday	Tuesday	Wednesday

Month of _____

Thursday	Friday	Saturday	Notes

Month of

Monthly To-Dos

Theme:

Top Goals:

Monthly One-Page Planner

Month of
_____

Top 5 Goals This Month

Goals

Financial Goals:

Marketing Goals:

Relationship Goals:

Monthly To-Dos:

Projects

Projects TO START this month:

Projects TO COMPLETE this month:

Projects TO CONTINUE this month:

Key Tasks for the Week of:

Week 1	Week 2	Week 3	Week 4	Week 5

Key Habits to Lean into:

This month will be a wild success when:

The Month in Focus

Month of
_____

	Week 1	Week 2	Week 3	Week 4
Key Priorities				
Key Successes				
Enablers				
Derailers				
Lessons Learned				
Next week I will…				

Monthly Daily Tracker

Month of _____

Day											
1											
2											
3											
4											
5											
6											
7											
8											
9											
10											
11											
12											
13											
14											
15											
16											
17											
18											
19											
20											
21											
22											
23											
24											
25											
26											
27											
28											
29											
30											
31											

Top Priorities

Notes

Taking Stock — Monthly Reflections

Month of
_____

Achievements:

Key Metrics (Finances/Numbers)

Income:

Expenses:

Social Media:

Marketing:

Other:

What worked this month:

What didn't:

Opportunities:

Obstacles:

Key Learning:

Relationships

Who helped me:

Relationships I need to cultivate:

Relationships that need attention:

Projects

Completed:

Still in process:

New/On Horizon:

Looking Ahead to the Next Month

Lessons learned and changes:

What I want to do to support my vision:

Top priorities:

Monthly Plan for

_____

Monthly Calendar

Sunday	Monday	Tuesday	Wednesday

Month of _____

Thursday	Friday	Saturday	Notes

Month of
_____

Monthly To-Dos

Theme:

Top Goals:

Monthly One-Page Planner

Month of
_____

Top 5 Goals This Month

Goals

Financial Goals:

Marketing Goals:

Relationship Goals:

Monthly To-Dos:

Projects

Projects TO START this month:

Projects TO COMPLETE this month:

Projects TO CONTINUE this month:

Key Tasks for the Week of:

Week 1	Week 2	Week 3	Week 4	Week 5

Key Habits to Lean into:

This month will be a wild success when:

The Month in Focus

Month of
_____

	Week 1	Week 2	Week 3	Week 4
Key Priorities				
Key Successes				
Enablers				
Derailers				
Lessons Learned				
Next week I will...				

Monthly Daily Tracker

Month of _____

Day										
1										
2										
3										
4										
5										
6										
7										
8										
9										
10										
11										
12										
13										
14										
15										
16										
17										
18										
19										
20										
21										
22										
23										
24										
25										
26										
27										
28										
29										
30										
31										

Top Priorities

Notes

Taking Stock – Monthly Reflections

Month of
_____

Achievements:

Key Metrics (Finances/Numbers)

Income:

Expenses:

Social Media:

Marketing:

Other:

Relationships

Who helped me:

Relationships I need to cultivate:

Relationships that need attention:

What worked this month:

What didn't:

Opportunities:

Obstacles:

Key Learning:

Projects

Completed:

Still in process:

New/On Horizon:

Looking Ahead to the Next Month

Lessons learned and changes:

What I want to do to support my vision:

Top priorities:

Monthly Plan for

_____

Monthly Calendar

Sunday	Monday	Tuesday	Wednesday

Month of _____

Thursday	Friday	Saturday	Notes

Month of
_____

Monthly To-Dos

Theme:

Top Goals:

Monthly One-Page Planner

Month of
_____

Top 5 Goals This Month

Goals

Financial Goals:

Marketing Goals:

Relationship Goals:

Monthly To-Dos:

Projects

Projects TO START this month:

Projects TO COMPLETE this month:

Projects TO CONTINUE this month:

Key Tasks for the Week of:

Week 1	Week 2	Week 3	Week 4	Week 5

Key Habits to Lean into:

This month will be a wild success when:

The Month in Focus

Month of
_____

	Week 1	Week 2	Week 3	Week 4
Key Priorities				
Key Successes				
Enablers				
Derailers				
Lessons Learned				
Next week I will…				

Monthly Daily Tracker

Month of _____

Day												
1												
2												
3												
4												
5												
6												
7												
8												
9												
10												
11												
12												
13												
14												
15												
16												
17												
18												
19												
20												
21												
22												
23												
24												
25												
26												
27												
28												
29												
30												
31												

Top Priorities

Notes

Taking Stock – Monthly Reflections

Month of
_____

Achievements:

Key Metrics (Finances/Numbers)

Income:

Expenses:

Social Media:

Marketing:

Other:

What worked this month:

What didn't:

Opportunities:

Obstacles:

Key Learning:

Relationships

Who helped me:

Relationships I need to cultivate:

Relationships that need attention:

Projects

Completed:

Still in process:

New/On Horizon:

Looking Ahead to the Next Month

Lessons learned and changes:

What I want to do to support my vision:

Top priorities:

Monthly Plan for

_____

Monthly Calendar

Sunday	Monday	Tuesday	Wednesday

Month of _____

Thursday	Friday	Saturday	Notes

Month of

Monthly To-Dos

Theme:

Top Goals:

Monthly One-Page Planner

Month of
_____

Top 5 Goals This Month

Goals

Financial Goals:

Marketing Goals:

Relationship Goals:

Monthly To-Dos:

Projects

Projects TO START this month:

Projects TO COMPLETE this month:

Projects TO CONTINUE this month:

Key Tasks for the Week of:

Week 1	Week 2	Week 3	Week 4	Week 5

Key Habits to Lean into:

This month will be a wild success when:

The Month in Focus

Month of

_____

	Week 1	Week 2	Week 3	Week 4
Key Priorities				
Key Successes				
Enablers				
Derailers				
Lessons Learned				
Next week I will...				

Monthly Daily Tracker

Month of _____

Day										
1										
2										
3										
4										
5										
6										
7										
8										
9										
10										
11										
12										
13										
14										
15										
16										
17										
18										
19										
20										
21										
22										
23										
24										
25										
26										
27										
28										
29										
30										
31										

Top Priorities

Notes

Taking Stock – Monthly Reflections

Month of
_____

Achievements:

Key Metrics (Finances/Numbers)

Income:

Expenses:

Social Media:

Marketing:

Other:

What worked this month:

What didn't:

Opportunities:

Obstacles:

Key Learning:

Relationships

Who helped me:

Relationships I need to cultivate:

Relationships that need attention:

Projects

Completed:

Still in process:

New/On Horizon:

Looking Ahead to the Next Month

Lessons learned and changes:

What I want to do to support my vision:

Top priorities:

Monthly Plan for

Monthly Calendar

Sunday	Monday	Tuesday	Wednesday

Month of _____

Thursday	Friday	Saturday	Notes

Month of
_____

Monthly To-Dos

Theme:

Top Goals:

Monthly One-Page Planner

Month of
_____

Top 5 Goals This Month

Goals

Financial Goals:

Marketing Goals:

Relationship Goals:

Monthly To-Dos:

Projects

Projects TO START this month:

Projects TO COMPLETE this month:

Projects TO CONTINUE this month:

Key Tasks for the Week of:

Week 1	Week 2	Week 3	Week 4	Week 5

Key Habits to Lean into:

This month will be a wild success when:

The Month in Focus

Month of
_____

	Week 1	Week 2	Week 3	Week 4
Key Priorities				
Key Successes				
Enablers				
Derailers				
Lessons Learned				
Next week I will…				

Monthly Daily Tracker

Month of _____

Day										
1										
2										
3										
4										
5										
6										
7										
8										
9										
10										
11										
12										
13										
14										
15										
16										
17										
18										
19										
20										
21										
22										
23										
24										
25										
26										
27										
28										
29										
30										
31										

Top Priorities

Notes

Taking Stock — Monthly Reflections

Month of
_____

Achievements:

Key Metrics (Finances/Numbers)

Income:

Expenses:

Social Media:

Marketing:

Other:

What worked this month:

What didn't:

Opportunities:

Obstacles:

Key Learning:

Relationships

Who helped me:

Relationships I need to cultivate:

Relationships that need attention:

Projects

Completed:

Still in process:

New/On Horizon:

Looking Ahead to the Next Month

Lessons learned and changes:

What I want to do to support my vision:

Top priorities:

Content Planning Tools

Content Brainstorming

Content Planner — Annual Overview

January	February	March
April	**May**	**June**
July	**August**	**September**
October	**November**	**December**

Monthly Content Tracker

Month of:_____

Day						
1						
2						
3						
4						
5						
6						
7						
8						
9						
10						
11						
12						
13						
14						
15						
16						
17						
18						
19						
20						
21						
22						
23						
24						
25						
26						
27						
28						
29						
30						
31						

Themes:

Notes:

Monthly Content Journal – One Line a Day

Month of:_____   Theme:_____

Use the One Line a Day to Capture Content/Ideas/Reflections

Day	
1	
2	
3	
4	
5	
6	
7	
8	
9	
10	
11	
12	
13	
14	
15	
16	
17	
18	
19	
20	
21	
22	
23	
24	
25	
26	
27	
28	
29	
30	
31	

Monthly Content Tracker

Month of:_____

Day						
1						
2						
3						
4						
5						
6						
7						
8						
9						
10						
11						
12						
13						
14						
15						
16						
17						
18						
19						
20						
21						
22						
23						
24						
25						
26						
27						
28						
29						
30						
31						

Themes:

Notes:

Monthly Content Journal – One Line a Day

Month of:_____

Theme:_____

Use the One Line a Day to Capture Content/Ideas/Reflections

Day	
1	
2	
3	
4	
5	
6	
7	
8	
9	
10	
11	
12	
13	
14	
15	
16	
17	
18	
19	
20	
21	
22	
23	
24	
25	
26	
27	
28	
29	
30	
31	

Monthly Content Tracker

Month of:_____

Day					
1					
2					
3					
4					
5					
6					
7					
8					
9					
10					
11					
12					
13					
14					
15					
16					
17					
18					
19					
20					
21					
22					
23					
24					
25					
26					
27					
28					
29					
30					
31					

Themes:

Notes:

Monthly Content Journal – One Line a Day

Month of:_____

Theme:_____

Use the One Line a Day to Capture Content/Ideas/Reflections

Day	
1	
2	
3	
4	
5	
6	
7	
8	
9	
10	
11	
12	
13	
14	
15	
16	
17	
18	
19	
20	
21	
22	
23	
24	
25	
26	
27	
28	
29	
30	
31	

Monthly Content Tracker

Month of:_____

Day						
1						
2						
3						
4						
5						
6						
7						
8						
9						
10						
11						
12						
13						
14						
15						
16						
17						
18						
19						
20						
21						
22						
23						
24						
25						
26						
27						
28						
29						
30						
31						

Themes:

Notes:

Monthly Content Journal – One Line a Day

Month of:_____

Theme:_____

Use the One Line a Day to Capture Content/Ideas/Reflections

Day	
1	
2	
3	
4	
5	
6	
7	
8	
9	
10	
11	
12	
13	
14	
15	
16	
17	
18	
19	
20	
21	
22	
23	
24	
25	
26	
27	
28	
29	
30	
31	

Monthly Content Tracker

Month of:_____

Day						
1						
2						
3						
4						
5						
6						
7						
8						
9						
10						
11						
12						
13						
14						
15						
16						
17						
18						
19						
20						
21						
22						
23						
24						
25						
26						
27						
28						
29						
30						
31						

Themes:

Notes:

Monthly Content Journal – One Line a Day

Month of:_____   Theme:_____

Use the One Line a Day to Capture Content/Ideas/Reflections

Day	
1	
2	
3	
4	
5	
6	
7	
8	
9	
10	
11	
12	
13	
14	
15	
16	
17	
18	
19	
20	
21	
22	
23	
24	
25	
26	
27	
28	
29	
30	
31	

Monthly Content Tracker

Month of:_____

Day						
1						
2						
3						
4						
5						
6						
7						
8						
9						
10						
11						
12						
13						
14						
15						
16						
17						
18						
19						
20						
21						
22						
23						
24						
25						
26						
27						
28						
29						
30						
31						

Themes:

Notes:

Monthly Content Journal – One Line a Day

Month of:_____   Theme:_____

Use the One Line a Day to Capture Content/Ideas/Reflections

Day	
1	
2	
3	
4	
5	
6	
7	
8	
9	
10	
11	
12	
13	
14	
15	
16	
17	
18	
19	
20	
21	
22	
23	
24	
25	
26	
27	
28	
29	
30	
31	

Monthly Content Tracker

Month of:_____

Day						
1						
2						
3						
4						
5						
6						
7						
8						
9						
10						
11						
12						
13						
14						
15						
16						
17						
18						
19						
20						
21						
22						
23						
24						
25						
26						
27						
28						
29						
30						
31						

Themes:

Notes:

Monthly Content Journal – One Line a Day

Month of:_____

Theme:_____

Use the One Line a Day to Capture Content/Ideas/Reflections

Day	
1	
2	
3	
4	
5	
6	
7	
8	
9	
10	
11	
12	
13	
14	
15	
16	
17	
18	
19	
20	
21	
22	
23	
24	
25	
26	
27	
28	
29	
30	
31	

Monthly Content Tracker

Month of:_____

Day						
1						
2						
3						
4						
5						
6						
7						
8						
9						
10						
11						
12						
13						
14						
15						
16						
17						
18						
19						
20						
21						
22						
23						
24						
25						
26						
27						
28						
29						
30						
31						

Themes:

Notes:

Monthly Content Journal – One Line a Day

Month of:_____

Theme:_____

Use the One Line a Day to Capture Content/Ideas/Reflections

Day	
1	
2	
3	
4	
5	
6	
7	
8	
9	
10	
11	
12	
13	
14	
15	
16	
17	
18	
19	
20	
21	
22	
23	
24	
25	
26	
27	
28	
29	
30	
31	

Monthly Content Tracker

Month of:_____

Day						
1						
2						
3						
4						
5						
6						
7						
8						
9						
10						
11						
12						
13						
14						
15						
16						
17						
18						
19						
20						
21						
22						
23						
24						
25						
26						
27						
28						
29						
30						
31						

Themes:

Notes:

Monthly Content Journal – One Line a Day

Month of:_____   Theme:_____

Use the One Line a Day to Capture Content/Ideas/Reflections

Day	
1	
2	
3	
4	
5	
6	
7	
8	
9	
10	
11	
12	
13	
14	
15	
16	
17	
18	
19	
20	
21	
22	
23	
24	
25	
26	
27	
28	
29	
30	
31	

Monthly Content Tracker

Month of:_____

Day					
1					
2					
3					
4					
5					
6					
7					
8					
9					
10					
11					
12					
13					
14					
15					
16					
17					
18					
19					
20					
21					
22					
23					
24					
25					
26					
27					
28					
29					
30					
31					

Themes:

Notes:

Monthly Content Journal – One Line a Day

Month of:_____

Theme:_____

Use the One Line a Day to Capture Content/Ideas/Reflections

Day	
1	
2	
3	
4	
5	
6	
7	
8	
9	
10	
11	
12	
13	
14	
15	
16	
17	
18	
19	
20	
21	
22	
23	
24	
25	
26	
27	
28	
29	
30	
31	

Monthly Content Tracker

Month of: _____

Day					
1					
2					
3					
4					
5					
6					
7					
8					
9					
10					
11					
12					
13					
14					
15					
16					
17					
18					
19					
20					
21					
22					
23					
24					
25					
26					
27					
28					
29					
30					
31					

Themes:

Notes:

Monthly Content Journal – One Line a Day

Month of:_____

Theme:_____

Use the One Line a Day to Capture Content/Ideas/Reflections

Day	
1	
2	
3	
4	
5	
6	
7	
8	
9	
10	
11	
12	
13	
14	
15	
16	
17	
18	
19	
20	
21	
22	
23	
24	
25	
26	
27	
28	
29	
30	
31	

Monthly Content Tracker

Month of:_____

Day						
1						
2						
3						
4						
5						
6						
7						
8						
9						
10						
11						
12						
13						
14						
15						
16						
17						
18						
19						
20						
21						
22						
23						
24						
25						
26						
27						
28						
29						
30						
31						

Themes:

Notes:

Monthly Content Journal – One Line a Day

Month of:_____

Theme:_____

Use the One Line a Day to Capture Content/Ideas/Reflections

Day	
1	
2	
3	
4	
5	
6	
7	
8	
9	
10	
11	
12	
13	
14	
15	
16	
17	
18	
19	
20	
21	
22	
23	
24	
25	
26	
27	
28	
29	
30	
31	

31-Day Challenge

1	2	3	4	5
6	7	8	9	10
11	12	13	14	15
16	17	18	19	20
21	22	23	24	25
26	27	28	29	30
31	Notes			

Content Collaboration Plan

Use the following to identify collaborators you can work with to help you get your content out.

Name	Details about their work and reach	How and why collaborate	What can I offer

Don't Just Do It Once! Scaling Content

Don't just do it once! Repurpose and republish is part of scaling your content and expanding your reach. Use this to identify possible posts you can repurpose and republish, and what that can look like.

Content I have created	Repurposing could include	Republishing could look like

Future Content Ideas

The Back Pages –
Creative Planning Tools

Ideas for Next Time

	January	February	March
Quarter 1			

	April	May	June
Quarter 2			

	July	August	September
Quarter 3			

	October	November	December
Quarter 4			

Brainstorming Sheet

Great Ideas to Action

One Page Plan

Goal	Description	Key Timelines	Resources (Who and What)	Enablers/Derailers

Daily Planner

Date _____ / _____ / _____

Schedule

6 AM	
7 AM	
8 AM	
9 AM	
10 AM	
11 AM	
12 PM	
1 PM	
2 PM	
3 PM	
4 PM	
5 PM	
6 PM	
7 PM	
8 PM	
9 PM	
10 PM	

Business Notes

Top 5 Goals

1.

2.

3.

4.

5.

To-Dos

About the Author

Jennifer Britton, MES, CHRL, CPT, PCC is the author of *Effective Group Coaching* (Wiley, 2010); *From One to Many: Best Practices for Team and Group Coaching* (Jossey-Bass, 2013) and *Effective Virtual Conversations: Engaging Digital Dialogue for Better Learning, Relationships, and Results.* (Potentials Realized Media, 2017) An expert in the area of group coaching and team development and a performance improvement specialist, she founded her company, Potentials Realized, in 2004. Since early 2006, her Group Coaching Essentials teleseminar program has supported hundreds of coaches in the creation and implementation of their own group coaching practice.

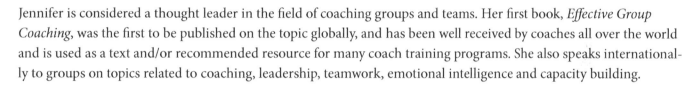

An award-winning program designer, Jennifer is dedicated to supporting groups, teams and organizations in the areas of leadership, teamwork and performance. She draws on more than two decades of experience as an experiential educator and former manager with the United Nations and other humanitarian organizations, with a global client list that spans government, corporate and nonprofit sectors, from financial services to education and healthcare.

Jennifer is considered a thought leader in the field of coaching groups and teams. Her first book, *Effective Group Coaching*, was the first to be published on the topic globally, and has been well received by coaches all over the world and is used as a text and/or recommended resource for many coach training programs. She also speaks internationally to groups on topics related to coaching, leadership, teamwork, emotional intelligence and capacity building.

Credentialed by the International Coaching Federation, Britton was originally trained and certified by the Coaches Training Institute. She has also completed advanced coaching training in the areas of ORSC and Shadow Coaching. A Certified Performance Technologist (CPT), Britton holds a Masters of Environmental Studies (York University) and a Bachelor of Science in Psychology (McGill).

Jennifer divides her time between just north of Toronto in East Gwillimbury, Ontario, and beautiful Muskoka, where she enjoys her next passion—nature—with her family.

EMAIL:
info@PotentialsRealized.com

WEBSITES:
www.CoachingBusinessBuilder.com

www.EffectiveVirtualConversations.com

www.PotentialsRealized.com

www.GroupCoachingEssentials.com

SOCIAL MEDIA:
Facebook: www.facebook.com/EffectiveGroupCoaching

Twitter: www.twitter.com/jennbritton

LinkedIn: www.linkedin.com/in/jenniferjbritton

Pinterest: www.pinterest.com/jennjbritton

You Tube: www.youtube.com/user/effectivegroupcoach

Check out the Coaching Biz Growth Lab™ for ongoing business development support in a group setting. www.CoachingBizGrowthLab.com.